Advance Praise

"Our research shows that purpose is something you're willing to make a sacrifice for, something that's bigger than you. The great paradox of purpose is that those who do so end up with richer lives, and it turns out that's just as true with companies and communities. The core truth of this book is that if you want an amazing life, give it to someone else."

Dr Vivienne Ming, Executive Chair and Co-Founder, Socos Labs

"After decades of dehumanizing work for the sake of increased shareholder value, this is one of the first books that puts humans at the centre stage of organizations. The shift from a cold mission to a purpose-driven organization that favours caring is a major change in leadership. The authors provide lots of practical tools and great examples of how to make this shift. A must-read book for leaders that want to succeed in our fast-changing world."

Antonio Nieto-Rodriguez, Global champion of project management, Thinkers50 award winner, author, *The Project Revolution* and *The Focused Organization*

"Connecting business with humanity and purpose is essential for leaders today. This must-read book eloquently captures the art and science of getting that right."

Anita Fleming, General Manager People & Culture, Kinrise

Published by
LID Publishing Limited
The Record Hall, Studio 304,
16-16a Baldwins Gardens,
London EC1N 7RJ, UK

info@lidpublishing.com
www.lidpublishing.com

A member of:

BPR

businesspublishersroundtable.com

© Sudhanshu Palsule & Michael Chavez, 2020
© LID Publishing Limited, 2020
Reprinted in 2020

Printed in Latvia by Jelgavas Tipogrāfija
ISBN: 978-1-911498-84-1

Cover design: Matthew Renaudin
Page design: Caroline Li

SUDHANSHU PALSULE
MICHAEL CHAVEZ

Rehumanizing Leadership

Putting Purpose Back into Business

MADRID | MEXICO CITY | LONDON
NEW YORK | BUENOS AIRES
BOGOTA | SHANGHAI | NEW DELHI

Dedication

The authors would like to dedicate this book to all those of you who have been participants on our programmes; to our clients from across the world; to our educators; and to Duke Corporate Education employees. All of you have inspired us to undertake this project through your deep curiosity and your thoughtful, authentic and heartfelt dialogue.

We also dedicate this book to those future researchers and writers who are inspired to delve more deeply into a topic that we believe will define leadership in the 21st century.

Acknowledgments

Writing this book has been a study in generosity. We would like to thank all those executives and subject-matter experts who agreed enthusiastically to be interviewed and offer their personal insights. We would have liked to have included quotes from every person whom we interviewed for this project, however, each of you graciously gave us insight and stories that were instrumental to our writing.

Our deepest gratitude goes to: James Alexander, Co-founder of Zopa and Voicefortheplanet.org; Lara Yumi Tsuji Bezerra, Chief Purpose Officer (Managing Director) at Roche Pharma India; Cathy Butler, Head of Executive Development at the Møller Institute, Kevin Cox, Chief Human Resources Officer of GE, formerly CHRO of American Express; Alex Edmans, Professor of Finance at London Business School; Shayne Elliott, Chief Executive Officer of ANZ; Pascal Finette, Chair for Entrepreneurship at Singularity University; Anita Fleming, General Manager People & Culture at Kinrise, formerly the Executive Manager, Group Strategy at ANZ; Jayne-Anne Gadhia, former CEO of Virgin Money and CEO of Salesforce UK, Frank Guglielmo, Managing Director at Park Consulting; Patrick Hull, HR and Strategy Director, Unilever; Elsbeth Johnson, Senior Lecturer at MIT Sloan;

George Kellar, Executive Director of the Zen Hospice Project; Tom Klein, Chief Marketing Officer at Mailchimp; Steve LaChance, Senior Vice President, LPL Financial; Adriana Marais, explorer and physicist; Vivienne Ming, Co-founder of Socos; Tim Munden, Chief Learning Officer at Unilever; Mfundo Nkuhlu, Chief Operating Officer at Nedbank; Denise Pickett, Chief Risk Officer and President, Global Risk, Banking and Compliance at American Express; Daniel Pink, author; Paul Polman, retired Chief Executive Officer at Unilever; James Prior, Global Head of Leadership Development at Novartis; Rosanna Ramos-Velita, Chairman of the Board of Caja Rural Los Andes; Antonio Nieto-Rodriguez, author; Gillian Secrett, Chief Executive Officer at the Møller Institute; Ant Strong, Group General Manager, Group Strategy at ANZ; Robi Supriyanto, musician and activist; Deborah Wahl, Global Chief Marketing Officer at Cadillac; Ewa Wojkowska, Chief Operating Officer at Kopernik; and Swati Yadav, Director of People and Culture at Roche Pharma India.

Through our work with them, our clients served as a wellspring of inspiration, insight and support on this project. Their kindness and openness inspired us to work harder and strive for more. At Roche, we would like to thank Severin Schwan and Silvia Ayyoubi for catalyzing a leadership movement at Roche that sparked the idea for this book. Thanks also to Stephanie Mitchell and Tammy Lowry for their support and feedback that made our work at Roche one of the high points of our careers.

We owe enormous thanks to many individuals at ANZ for their generosity in involving us in ANZ's purpose story. We are grateful to the entire extended leadership team at ANZ who enthusiastically shared their thinking and perspectives.

At Astellas, thanks to Lisa Gray, Angie Keister, Sean Penistone, Kathy Schroeder and Norio Suzuki, fellow practitioners who trusted us to experiment and helped us shape our point of view. Thanks also to the Executive Team at Astellas who singularly and collectively model purposeful leadership.

We would like to thank Sean Hartley, Carla Mahieu and Alex Wynaendts at AEGON who showed us tremendous trust and support early on in this endeavour by encouraging courageous discussions on purpose among their leaders.

At American Express, we would like to offer our thanks to Jaclyn Wood, Mayra Garcia-Egan, Michelle Bal, Samantha Hammock and Greg Hybl who have been outstanding partners and have helped us to raise our thinking to a new level.

To our publishers at LID, we thank you for your belief in us and in your deep and authentic partnership. Thanks especially to Niki Mullin, Ben Walker, Patrick Woodman, Susan Furber, and Matthew Renaudin.

We are fortunate to be able to work at Duke Corporate Education, a place that has sustained us and energized us throughout our careers. To each and every one of our colleagues and educators, we thank you for your support, thoughtfulness, curiosity and encouragement. We owe an unpayable debt to Duke CE's marketing team, especially to Christine Robers and Kevin Anselmo for serving as the engine room of this project, never losing sight of the details and yet always staying focused on the bigger purpose of this work and of the work we do with clients.

To anyone we may have inadvertently omitted, please accept our apologies and our heartfelt thanks.

Contents

Prologue

The Two Vectors of Evolution

The last upgrade that the human brain went through in our evolution as a species was the development of the pre-frontal cortex, approximately 70,000 years ago. The development of this new brain instantly separated us from all other species. Homo sapiens began marching to a very different beat of evolution and human cultures began to take shape through the medium of language and an ability to communicate in increasingly sophisticated ways. The pre-frontal cortex evolved loaded with the capacity for memory and consequently an ability to conceive of time as past, present and future. We were able to now operate simultaneously on two cognitive levels: reality and imagined reality. Free to think of 'what could be', humankind rose to the top of the food chain and began transforming the environment to make it more amenable for survival. Imagination, or as cognitive scientists term it, 'represented reality', brought with it the complex need for purpose, something that was hitherto unnecessary in the scheme of things. The need for purpose has arguably been one of the most powerful vectors of evolution. Not just satisfied with what is, but the need to know the reason why, has been the source of extraordinary development in almost every aspect of existence, from philosophy, science, technology and medicine to literature, art and poetry in every civilization in the world. Purpose became an important tool for human beings to devise more sophisticated ways to thrive in the hostile climate of sub-Saharan Africa. Seeking out purpose emerged as a fitness-enhancing adaptation as it allowed for group cohesiveness. In that sense, purpose is hardwired into our consciousness as an evolutionary mechanism. Life itself may or may not be purposeful, but the need for purpose is, nonetheless, a powerful human need.

The complexities of developing relationships led to the development of another vector, that of empathy. Along with the need for purpose, this marked a major evolutionary breakthrough in the development of the human brain. As neuroscientists put it, the 'computational requirements' of dealing with a hostile environment and the need to inter-act and communicate with others sculpted the empathetic function. Empathizing with the other is a highly complex evolutionary ability requiring a sophisticated coordina-tion between our sensory systems (detecting feelings) and emotional systems (mirroring emotions). When infants cry at the recorded sounds of other infants or when our tear ducts involuntarily produce tears at the sight of another's suffering, it demonstrates how an ancient adaptive ability to empathize continues to throb inside the brain.

Arianna Huffington, who founded *The Huffington Post*, once did an interview with Edwin Rutsch in which she referred to her moment of insight while talking to Jonas Salk, before Salk's passing in 1995. Salk had defined the transitional period we are in as moving from an epoch based on survival and competition to a new epoch that must nec-essarily be based on collaboration and meaning. This was the moment of Huffington's epiphany: that empathy was not to be perceived as that "quaint behaviour to be trotted out during intermittent holiday visits to the food bank."[1]

That insight went into a book called *The Fourth Instinct*[2] in which Huffington explored the instinct that takes us beyond the first three human impulses for survival, sex and power and drives us to expand the boundaries of our caring to include our communities and the world around us. That instinct is just as vital as the other three impulses, but we rarely give it the same kind of attention. Paul Polman, who recently retired as Chief Executive Officer (CEO) of Unilever, simply calls it caring: caring for the larger context that goes beyond mere profits. For Huffington, empathy lies at the very core of human existence: "A value that is vital both on the small personal scale and the large public scale". Huffington draws an evocative analogy between the interconnected networks of digital technology and the interconnection that is required at the human level. AI is starting to make the trillion-node network possible; empathy does the same for human beings. Making her point here, Huffington says, "And if we don't acknowledge that and base our decisions on it, we are going to be in major trouble ... I believe empathy is the one quality we most need to teach and nurture if we're going to survive and flourish in the 21st Century."

The two vectors of purpose and empathy were responsible for the creation of meaning as a crucial turning point in our development as a species. The quest for meaning would go on to become one of the most important requirements for the human brain. Many people tend to view purpose and meaning as interchangeable words but in reality they mean entirely different things. Meaning is the result of putting our purpose and our ability to empathize to work into a larger context, something that is much larger than we are. We tend to think of meaning as something to be found and to be held on to; on the contrary, it is exactly the opposite. Meaning appears when we find ourselves making a positive difference; when our lives and work become meaningful to the other. That is precisely why meaning only occurs in the act of relationship, it is not a solitary activity. Interestingly, it only manifests itself in the act of giving rather than taking! Consequently, we feel a loss of meaning when we find ourselves not contributing or being of service.

The 'dark night of the soul' is a term that writers have used to label precisely such a crisis, one that often takes place in our lives after we have achieved success in the traditional material sense. You could refer to it as the freeway moment: that time when you are stuck in a traffic jam at 8.30pm on a dark, rainy Thursday evening. You've had days and days of running around in circles and meetings with no positive impact and little time spent with loved ones. Despite the fact that you have a job you fought hard to get, a very healthy bank balance, and a wonderful home in the suburbs, the one question that looms large as you watch the wipers swish away in the night is: 'what am I doing with my life?'

If meaning is so important to us as a species, why do we not protect it as a resource? Interestingly, the same upgrade in our brains that evolved the need for meaning also evolved into what neuroscientist and philosopher Francisco Varela termed 'know-how', the conditioned autopilot through which we navigate our way through life. Anthropologist Pierre Bourdieu calls it the 'habitus', the way in which our deepest tendencies are constrained by the cultural environment in which we exist.

Quite unconsciously, we are conditioned in our societies to subscribe to the dominant narratives of our age and culture. Therefore, concepts such as survival of the fittest become the cultural template that condition us to believe in the fang and claw model in which everyone is out to look after themselves. In fact, if you were to examine the dominant mythologies that have shaped our understanding of ourselves, our thinking and behaviour over the past few hundred years, you would find we have largely put individual interests before anything else. In the process, we have become dehumanized to our natural environment and to the wider communities in which we exist.

We – the authors – feel rather strongly, that this narrative has reached the end of its usefulness for two key reasons.

First, the very environment that keeps us alive has overshot the limits of sustainability. Global warming is but one example. Realities such as the devastation of our natural ecosystems through toxic waste like plastics, and the inability of our environment to support the growing population are tearing apart the very flawed logic of seeing ourselves as separate from nature. We need an urgent shift in thinking for our very survival. Second, we now live in a complex and interconnected world fueled by digital technology and global information flows. Wired up like a gigantic network, the 21st century is rendering old mythologies of nation states and the 'us-versus-them' mindset that was a manifestation of a more tribal world obsolete.

Biologist Edward O. Wilson has written about how our evolution from tribal to global societies increasingly favours compassion over callous and competitive human interaction. Complex problems such as global warming simply cannot be solved unless we learn to collaborate and approach the problems from a systems perspective.

The gap between a 21st century hyper-networked world of interconnections and interdependencies with an unprecedented ability for mass collaboration and our pre-industrial age mindset has become alarmingly large. 'Unconscious Capitalism', to play on Mackey and Sisodia's excellent work on *Conscious Capitalism*,[3] has warped that mindset even more. The result is a worldview in which our very sense of self and of our organizations is dangerously separated from our societies and our environment.

Writing in *Psychology Today*, anthropologist Samuel Veissière refers to a dangerous 'sense of entitlement' that we have inherited. "It is our historical amnesia and geopolitical blindness that make us content, selfish and ignorant. Yet, we are not entitled to any of the privileges we take for granted.

More than our privileges, we owe our very life to humanity and the planet as a whole."[4]

It is time for us to completely transform the very foundations of our worldview. Ervin László wrote this in his classic work, *Evolution: The Grand Synthesis*, "Nothing that has ever emerged in this world – and that manages to persist in it – is exempt from further evolution. Not just life, even our organizations and societies are part of the evolutionary template. Nothing is outside of the grand story of evolution." Lazlo went on to write, "If human beings no longer seem to evolve as a biological species, they certainly do as members of human society; the leading edge of human evolution is no longer genetic ... it is determined ... by the presen ... Evolution is the maker of the future ..."[5]

We only have to observe nature to understand that there is a more viable, saner alternative to the exploitative model we have been following for some 500 odd years. Pick up a handful of soil and it is teeming with millions of bacteria and microorganisms that are working non-stop to maintain the life-support systems of our planet. Nature has a simple secret: life creates conditions for life so that life may thrive. If nature had operated from an entitlement perspective, life would simply not have evolved. Period.

This is the debt that we owe to our life support systems and to life itself; a debt that, as anthropologist David Graeber points out, can never be repaid. What we can do is to make sure we build and manage our organizations and societies from a genuinely new 21st century perspective that honours our long lineage. The two vectors of purpose and empathy that we carry embedded in our pre-frontal cortex are our resources for leadership in the 21st century.

We wrote this book as an invitation to you, the reader, to explore and practise a way of leadership that is in tune with the demands of the 21st century context, one that is defined by one word more than any other – complexity. In such a context, profit and purpose must go hand-in-hand and self-interest and caring for the other must work together. This will require us not just to understand the complexity of the 21st century, but also to transform the way we think. It also requires that we radically change our conception of leadership.

Rehumanizing leadership is about transforming our organizations to operate from the axes of purpose and empathy with a view to creating a meaningful impact on the external environment of nature, market and society, and in our workplaces.

And, it is about doing so in a disruptive and fast-moving 21st century where digital technology, global information flows and a new millennial demographic are rewriting the very rules of work, life and leadership.

In momentous times of great change, paradox is rife and everywhere. While digital technology is transforming our world into an interconnected whole, we are literally building walls of protectionism around us. A new politics of dehumanization and divisiveness is being legitimized by political leaders across the world, and we continue to push the planet beyond its carrying capacity. Historically, the period before any great change is always marked by two worldviews in friction, much like tectonic plates grating against each other. There is the last resistance of the irrelevant and then the system tips over.

Just as we were making final edits on this book, the first ever photograph of a black hole has been published. Christened 'Powehi', an Hawaiian phrase referring to an 'embellished dark source of unending creation', it is fitting that the task of creating a new algorithm for putting together

all the images that were created using computational tele-
scopes was done by a 30-year-old millennial and computer
scientist, Katie Bouman. Awe inspiring and mysterious, the
image of the black hole is a global epiphany for a new meaning about the fragile beauty of our planet and its species.
Much like the first image of planet Earth taken from the
Apollo 17 spacecraft in 1972, which went on to inspire generations to come, this image forces us to revisit the inescapable reality of humanity: survival is a collective effort. Seen
in this view, it is likely that this picture of a black hole, 55
million light years from Earth, is likely to become a defining
moment for the 21st century.

Part 1

Why Things Are The Way They Are

"The major problems in the world are the result of the difference between how nature works and the way people think."

GREGORY BATESON

CHAPTER 1

The 21ˢᵗ Century Imperative

"In the 20ᵗʰ century, the biggest challenge was some people exploiting other people. But in the 21ˢᵗ century, maybe the biggest conflict of all will be about irrelevance."

YUVAL NOAH HARARI

How do we stay relevant and significant in the 21ˢᵗ century? Information is becoming a commodity as access to it is becoming a level playing field. Technologies are converging so as to create disruptive possibilities that can emerge from anywhere and everywhere. Artificial intelligence, robotics and the Internet of Things (IoT) are creating a reality that transcends and challenges our 20ᵗʰ century assumptions. So many of our organizations – still carrying residues of the Industrial Revolution – are being dislocated by these gigantic technological shifts, with no clear indication of the emergent future. The debate over what role human beings will have in this emergent reality continues unresolved.

We are not futurists; however, our research points us toward the following hypotheses about the future:

1. Being human will matter even more in a world of digital technology
2. Questions of relevance and significance will become more important than ever before
3. Purpose, meaning and empathy are becoming the determinants of how we perform in a world of data, algorithms and artificial intelligence

However, the rehumanization of leadership is not about taking us back to some mythical past when everything was nice and human. It is not about turning the clock back to a better time. On the contrary, this rehumanization has to occur in the context of the reality of digital technology and globalization. We welcome the opportunities that digital technology is bringing about in creating a new landscape of transparency and trust. The rehumanization of leadership will include both the perennial aspects of what it means to be human and the new skills and capabilities that leadership will need in an increasingly networked world. For this, we will need new terminology, concepts and frameworks. As we start wading into the 21st century waters of digital technology, the need to rehumanize our leadership is becoming a matter of critical importance. Unlike the popular belief that digital technology will render people less important, we hold exactly the contrarian view.

Leadership by its very nature emerges out of relationships and that, necessarily, should make it a deeply humanizing process. But it seldom is, hence the title of this book. In fact, as we write this book the *Harvard Business Review* has come up with a series of publications called "How to be human at work". This is without any intended irony and clearly the editors at HBR have seen a need for this series.

A Growing Crisis of Meaning

We are starting to find ourselves in a world that is increasingly dislocating itself from the familiar. Global information flows and digital technologies, while creating exciting opportunities, are also opening up a chasm wide and deep between the world as we knew it until recently and the one that is emerging around us. Surrounded by big data, the promise of AI and the unceasing flow of information into the supercomputer we carry in our pockets and handbags, we are more confused than ever about the deeper questions that refuse to go away. Materially, many of us are better off as a whole than we have ever been before, but we seem more disconnected than ever from our context. The problems of falling water tables and climate change are now immediate issues and it is clear that we can no longer treat the planet as a waste sink.

Recently, in the UK more people watched the *Blue Planet* episode on plastics than any other television programme. Horrified, we watched plastic islands drifting through the blue oceans of our world, knowing our part in the vicious cycle of consumption and waste. What *Blue Planet* did, however, was to spearhead a growing outrage against plastic consumption, forcing manufacturers and retailers to rethink their use of plastics. Fast-moving consumer companies like Unilever and Procter & Gamble reported a spike in the uptake of purpose-led brands. Social media platforms allowed millions of consumers to voice their concerns, with a direct impact not only on corporate strategies but also on the fundamental ways in which companies think about how they operate.

If the 2008 financial crisis threw out the skeletons in the corporate greed cupboard, creating public distrust in many of the implicated institutions, the situation today has become even more volatile. Facebook lost $120 billion in market cap in a single day.[6] People simply registered the importance of trust in how value is measured. It turns out that 60% of British people do not trust the institutions of business, governments, NGOs and media, according to the 2019 Edelman Trust Barometer.[7] Overall, there is little confidence in the institutions that govern our society and shape our future, as well as their ability to 'do the right thing'. The 2015 Nielsen Global Corporate Sustainability Report found that 66% of global consumers are willing to pay more for sustainable brands. Out of that, 73% of millennials are willing to pay extra for brands that are making a difference.[8] Some companies are starting to respond with innovative approaches to age-old business models.

Kopernik[9] is a not-for-profit R&D lab for poverty reduction based in Indonesia. Their Chief Operating Officer, Ewa Wojkowska, and one of their partners, Robi Supriyanto, an activist and rock musician, shared with us their efforts to influence FMCG companies to reduce plastic waste in Indonesia: "It's not enough to just try to get companies to cut a product that generates plastic waste. We realized that if they do so, another company will simply fill the gap with another similar product. Instead, we're getting them to think about being a brand leader and publicly promoting the issue of plastic waste, as well as being part of the solution with new, innovative packaging. Through this we hope their competitors will see that the product has become a meaningful product to consumers and society and copy the solution."

The 21st century imperative for change manifests itself through four key factors: the challenge of complexity; the millennial stand; dealing with ambiguity; and the need for adaptability. Let's take a look at each one of these in some detail.

A. The Challenge of Complexity

The defining term for the 21st century – complexity – conjures up images of an unmanageable world in which disruption is the new normal and leaders had better adapt or perish. The fact is globalization, digitalization, converging technologies, and a new millennial mindset of transparency and collaboration are colluding to obliterate the illusion of a predictable future. All along we had assumed we could navigate the future using the trusted recipe of information, capability and strategy. In a survey by Duke CE, CEOs declared complexity as their number one challenge.[10]

But complexity is neither the problem nor a new phenomenon. Our Earth's life-support systems are highly complex, which explains their resilience for millennia!

The human brain is complex. Unlike the theories of the past in which we assumed that specific brain areas carried out certain functions, we now know that it operates in a very non-linear way. Any human group, including a family, is a complex system. So are traffic systems and insect swarms and bird clusters. Even the simplest living system – a bacterial cell – is a highly complex network involving literally thousands of interdependent chemical reactions.

The 21st century is radically challenging our belief in linearity. From global warming to global pricing policies, the linear walls that delineated competitors, governments, regulators and technologies into understandable boxes are crumbling in front of our eyes. Social media allows customers to talk to each other, access the same information and influence public opinion with a point of view. The customer is no longer the passive recipient. Yet, so many organizations continue to position leadership as an instrument for maximizing efficiency or output, so much so that we have come to accept that as the norm. We have to come up with an entirely new way of leading in the 21st century.

While the environment in which we work and lead operates as an interconnected, interdependent ecosystem, we continue to manage our 20th century organizations in a linear way. Top-down communication and ascribed power are becoming increasingly ineffective. So is the view of employees as instruments. As Leena Nair, Head of Human Resources at Unilever, said when we interviewed her, "Too often, leaders see employees as abstract talent – not real people. This is why everything I do is centred around our business being more human." What has always been an important factor in organizations has suddenly become critical in the 21st century. Leena referred to deeply human traits such as judgment, creativity, ingenuity and empathy becoming the key 21st century abilities. "These are also the very traits that the World Economic Forum has highlighted as becoming essential for future job roles."

As the business environment becomes increasingly complex and ambiguous, there is an even greater need to rehumanize leadership, imbuing it with deeper meaning and purpose.

B. The Millennial Stand

When researching for our previous book, *The Social Leader*,[11] along with co-author, Frank Guglielmo, we found that the two things that millennials value about work more than anything else were meaningful purpose and authenticity from their leaders. A recent study by PwC called *Workforce of the future: The Yellow World in 2030*[12] found that 88% of them want to work for a company whose values reflect their own. More tellingly, it is predicted that millennials will comprise 75% of the workforce in about seven to eight years.

The PwC report stated that 88% of millennials want to work for a company whose values reflect their own. Millennials are combining a search for personal fulfilment in their lives and careers with a search for meaningful work places. How long can companies pretend that issues of sustainability, gender-diversity and all the other issues that the millennials are upholding do not exist?

In a 2017 Davos roundtable meeting, Mark Weinberger, Chairman and CEO of EY, spoke about the need to learn from the big geopolitical events happening around the globe, and that business must focus on something longer than the bottom line. "Trying quarterly to quarterly to managing your numbers as against taking the larger picture and investing in the long run," as he described it. Weinberger is one of many CEO's already talking about doing well and doing good. According to Weinberger, 75% of EY's employees are millennials, and he talks of losing out if they do not address these people while putting their strategy together.

What is more, employees at a purpose-led business are up to three times more productive than the average workforce. Workers are far more enthusiastic and energetic when they know they are contributing to a bigger picture. It is no longer enough for businesses to appear socially ethical on the surface, they must now internalize and incorporate this purpose-driven attitude if they want to appeal to this empowered millennial workforce.

It does not take too much thinking to figure out why millennials are demanding purpose-led organizations and leadership:

1. A lack of trust in corporations and business following the 2008 financial crisis and a growing scepticism about large corporations and institutions

2. The technological ability to work from anywhere that provides greater choice about the kind of work they want to do. This is also because of the growing urbanization of the world that naturally provides more choice
3. Redefining work as a key lifestyle choice and even as a source of happiness rather than as a means of earning an income
4. Relevance and meaning are defined by the purpose and values of the organization and how closely they match those of the individual

Every now and then we get asked the same question: "Isn't this just a generational thing? Doesn't every generation come with different expectations and desires, and think that they are being unique?" Well, the answer is yes and no. Between the two of us as authors, we are children of the sixties and seventies. We saw the rebellion against the Vietnam War, the student riots, and the anti-establishment stand. The crucial difference was that our respective generations, the baby-boomers and generation X, never really controlled the technology that changes the world. This is the first time that a generation is going to be the one in charge of the technology that is changing the world. Moreover, the fact is this generation is starting to demand a rehumanization of the world and of the workplace.

C. Dealing with Ambiguity

Ambiguity comes across as an anomaly considering that the 21st century context is about the explosion of information. It is a mind-boggling fact that close to 100% of all information available today was put together in this century. Such is the exponential rise of information, and it is only going to get worse or better, depending on how you see it. The problem is not information, but how we make sense of it and decide what information is relevant, especially when everything is changing all the time. Ambiguity is the experience of *not knowing* despite the availability of information. As one senior executive in a 150-year-old insurance company said to us, "I have more information than I can handle, that's not the problem; I am struggling with the context. I just don't know where the next disruption is coming from. And I am struggling for time to make sense of all this."

One of the big problems of ambiguity is that the human brain does not do well in its presence. When faced with ambiguity, the brain resorts to operating from old and familiar biases and behaviours and the result is that the brain reacts rather than responds. We feel that one of the most important facets of rehumanizing leadership is about helping people productively deal with rising levels of ambiguity.

Ambiguity forces us to fundamentally change how organizations pick up information, create strategies and execute them. The typical 20th century approach of going from strategy to execution is based on the assumption that the world remains still enough while you are first formulating and then executing your strategy. Ambiguity forces us to adopt a completely different approach. How quickly we can learn and unlearn becomes more important than getting your strategy right. The same applies to the habits and knowledge we may have learned from the past. Porter's 'five forces' model of driving competitive advantage may continue to look neat and tidy, but the model is woefully inappropriate in a 21st century context of driving value in ecosystems.

The ability to quickly pick up weak signals from the environment and respond to them is fast becoming a mandatory requirement in the 21st century. As we shall see later in this book, 20th century organizations were built like fortifications and are ill-equipped to be responsive and agile. More porosity, fewer work levels, flat structures, intensive collaboration, creating ecosystem value and having a group of inspired value creators who are in close contact with the external environment is the only way to do this. Disruption is not a new phenomenon, but the scale and speed at which digital technology is able to disrupt existing environments, business models and markets certainly is. Small changes lead very quickly to rapid amplification and if the weak signals are not picked up early, it is already too late, as companies like Nokia discovered.

D. The Need for Adaptability

The 20th century organization was not built to be adaptable, far from it. Adaptability is different from managing change. Those of you who made your way up to top management in the era of change management in the 20th century will remember all the neat and tidy terms from the time. Gap analysis, SWOT analysis, freezing and unfreezing, and all the other change management tools that went into quite an elaborate industry that was set up in the previous century. The fact is that even in the 20th century change management had a dismal success record because human beings and organizations are not meant to be machines. But the trend continued for a long while, since it appeared to be rational and appealed to the mood of the time. Some of the executives we work with still shudder at the memory of all those change management workshops that went on for inordinately long lengths of time in closed rooms with a select few, while the rest of the organization waited for the information to be 'cascaded' down to them! Unless you have a nostalgia for those good old days when time stretched on, you would have a similar reaction.

The core assumption we used in the 20ᵗʰ century was that the world was knowable and certain, which is what made it possible for us to build and justify the fortified organization of the 20ᵗʰ century that could exist separately from the environment it was in, surrounded by hard, thick walls. Products and services could be shipped out through specific, traditional channels. We had terms like market intelligence, through which we tracked what the competition in the industry was doing. So Nokia continued to track Motorola as a rival even while Apple was rewriting the rules of the ecosystem. In an uncertain world, the fortified organization quickly loses touch with reality. Operating in ecosystems is very different from operating unilaterally with customers or with competition. In fact, the mindset required to operate in ecosystems is contrary to the one we learned to use in the 20ᵗʰ century. To receive you have to first give; fail to give and you risk becoming irrelevant!

When you get rid of this model of certainty and predictability and replace it with one in which the external environment is anything but known and certain, everything that we are used to doing in the 20ᵗʰ century starts breaking down. We become irrelevant. When we, the authors, consult to our more traditional clients in the finance, insurance, FMCG and pharmaceutical industries our conversations with their senior executives are largely about relevance. *"How long do you think you will stay relevant in the 21ˢᵗ century if you continue this way?"* is a great conversation starter! In a leadership workshop we recently ran for a well-known bank in the UK, the CEO replied, "If we are brutally honest, we are already irrelevant; it is only a matter of time." We then posed the following challenge: "If we gave you a ton of money to build a new bank from scratch, would it look like the bank you are managing right now?" We don't need to tell you what the answer was.

Then they went on to describe what the new bank would look like: flatter, agile, porous, nimble and quick to change. A nice wish list to have!

Another reason for needing to be adaptable is the level of scrutiny that every organization faces. There is literally no place to hide, as the authors of *The Social Leader* wrote. Our organizations are open to scrutiny with an increasing demand for transparency. Only an adaptable organization is able to quickly respond to external demands from stakeholders and customers, and internal demands from employees, especially millennials.

Together, the four factors of complexity, adaptability, ambiguity and a new millennial demographic are shaping the global landscape. Putting purpose back into business is no longer just wishful and charitable thinking. It is the 21st century code of relevance for organizations and for leadership.

Purpose: The Invisible Power of Leadership

Richard Branson wrote the foreword for Jayne-Anne Gadhia's 2018 book called *The Virgin Banker*,[13] in which she writes the story of how she and her team built Virgin Money as a business. Branson writes in the foreword, "I don't just want a bank that makes profit, I want a bank that creates experiences, builds relationships and enriches people's lives." Virgin Money challenged the archetypal banking sector and its formality and its foreboding hierarchies and power structures. We shall be looking at how Jayne-Anne used purposeful leadership as a key cornerstone of Virgin Money's success later in the book. The power of the Virgin brand comes from the one single purpose that Branson spells out with no hesitation: "... to make a positive difference to people's lives".

For the 20-odd years that Jayne-Anne was part of the Virgin group she has never felt any different, and the sense of purpose that has driven her and her teams has been unwavering.

Purpose is hardly a new phenomenon. One of the early exponents of purpose was the venerable Mary Parker Follet, who referred to purpose as being the *invisible leader* in highly effective companies. That was in 1928. Gill Robinson Hickman and Georgia Sorensen went on to develop this idea further, by referring to invisible leadership as "embodying situations in which dedication to a compelling and deeply held common purpose is the motivational force for leadership". In their book, *The Power of Invisible Leadership*,[14] Hickman and Sorenson refer to purpose as embodying "deeply meaningful shared experiences, beliefs, values and goals". Purpose may be invisible, but it is ever-present in everything we do. And when there is a crisis, or that moment of reckoning when answers are not easily available, the purpose provides a guide to action. That is why, as Hickman and Sorenson say, a purpose goes far beyond a mission statement. "It is a deeply held sense of common destiny, a life course or calling; it is aligned with a mission but resonates profoundly with people's values and their sense of themselves." We met Gill at a conference on purpose at the Møller Institute in Cambridge this year. When we asked her whether Follet's 1928 idea was still relevant, her answer was, "Absolutely. In fact, more so than ever before!"

In an evocative metaphor, Hickman and Sorenson compare purpose to the space between two notes in music. Listening to the 'blue notes' of Thelonius Monk is a stirring musical experience because of his mastery of the empty space between the notes. Every time any of the leaders we have been working with has been confronted by a crisis or a challenge, they have returned to that invisible force of purpose. As Hickman and

Sorenson write, "The invisible force becomes the space where inspiration, interaction and connection between a purpose and its leaders and followers ignite to bring about something extraordinary."

Motivation in a Digital World

One of the complaints we often hear about millennials is their lack of loyalty to the organization and their need to change jobs frequently. Research shows again and again that purpose is a far better glue to retain your best talent than any other factor. Second, as organizations become more lateral and as hierarchical authority and referral power diminishes, purpose becomes a key rallying point around which people coalesce. Finally, leading people over whom one has no formal authority is becoming the norm rather than the exception. In complex, global organizations, reporting lines no longer have the same meaning any more; purpose repeatedly trumps everything else.

With formal knowledge already becoming a commodity, a leader no longer has any disproportionate knowledge over the others. What that leaves leaders with is their passion, a powerful sense of purpose, their capacity for empathy and their ability to inspire meaning in others. Dave Packard, co-founder of Hewlett-Packard, was reported to have said in 1960,[15] "I want to discuss why a company exists in the first place. In other words, why are we here? I think many people assume wrongly that a company exists simply to make money." This is not a vision that Packard is referring to; a vision is something that expires and then a new one has to be set. Purpose, as an answer to a fundamental existential question, endures over time.

Overcoming the
Industrial Past

To rehumanize leadership, we will have to overcome an industrial age worldview that taught us to define ourselves and our organizations as closed and fragmented black boxes. This approach did seem to work well as long as the world functioned as a linear and a closed system. So strategy became the Holy Grail and the harbinger of success. And yes, every once in a while, we would pay lip service to our values, except those were not values at all but, at best, a list of aspirational statements that were unmoored from reality. At worst they were simply feel-good lines. Purpose had little or no value in a worldview that was defined by inputs and outputs. Our contention is that purpose will have to be the core leadership resource in the 21st century.

Human beings are essentially meaning makers; the higher emotions of purpose, empathy and shared meaning are critical as they build the foundations for sustainability. But like the proverbial one-eyed king in the country of the blind, strategy became king in the 20th century in the belief that as long as anything could be quantified it was seen as working. In fact we spent much of the 20th century assuming that measurement holds the secret to mastery. We set up countless cottage industries inside our companies devoted to the sole task of generating information and converting everything into smart decks, spreadsheets, graphs and statistics. Useful tools as long as they don't commandeer the central position in the complex system of meaning. But, sadly, that is precisely what happened.

Management became the science of finding the most efficient procedures to maximize production by designing the organization as an assemblage of clear, interlocking parts of functions, departments and processes that are managed by lines of command and control. Remember the catch-phrase 're-engineering the corporation' from the nineties? In fact, the complicated financial instruments at the core of the credit crisis of 2008 came out of computer models to reconstitute bad loans in ways that were meant to eliminate most of the risks. These models were wrong, but because they were quantified and looked smart we assumed they were right.[16] Purpose or intention had no place in these models. But greed and self-interest did.

The rehumanization of leadership has become one of the most pressing issues of our times. Two of our biggest clients, a leading pharmaceutical company and a successful global bank, have both been on a journey of over two years in doing precisely this, with very tangible rewards. We will be discussing their journey a bit later. For now, we want to put a placeholder on the three traps that we must watch out for. We will get back to these traps in detail in Chapter 6.

The Three Traps
The Control Trap

The biggest problem is that most 20th century organizations are simply not equipped to deal with this new reality. They were built on the assumption of a linear world; so we built neat looking boxes of departments, functions, hierarchies and reporting lines that allowed us to exercise control. Now we demand agility, adaptability and innovation from our employees, but we still reward them for status, obedience and conformity within the old, neat looking boxes.

The Cognitive Trap

Our brains are simply not adapted for complexity. Nature has prepared us for immediate danger and reacting instantly, but not for deciphering the weak signals of complex problems. Our brains lack the neural wiring to understand weak signals; this is a skill that must be learned. Ambiguity tends to appear as a threat, triggering an instant reaction which is inherently biased. That is why we would rather defend an established belief or strategy and ignore evidence to the contrary than ask if we are doing the right thing.

The Power Trap

The 20th century hierarchical organization was built to replicate social status and top-down power, which were achieved through the control of information and resources. But as the hierarchy itself comes under challenge from complex and lateral networks in equally complex ecosystems, this traditional source of power starts becoming irrelevant. Recent research in neurology also demonstrates how those who 'feel powerful' through social status have a lower ability to feel empathy. The 20th century organization engaged reward mechanisms in our brains to derive power from status; how willing are we to give that up?

The Wrong Mindsets

The control trap, the cognitive trap and the power trap can work together to produce a reactive mindset in individuals as well as collectively. This mindset propels us to act from old and often unconscious biases, emotional states and learned scripts without thinking. It is firmly rooted in a survival fight-or-flight mechanism. Needless to say, such a mindset is redundant when addressing complex problems.

While this survival mindset might be invaluable when faced with a charging rhinoceros in the African savannah, it is of no use whatsoever when we are managing a steel company in a global environment that is no longer conducive to business as usual. And yet, we see managers repeatedly falling into this trap of tackling complexity with a reactive mindset.

But don't we also have another mindset that is not reactive? One that acts much more logically and instead of instantaneously reacting to a situation is able to gather information and respond more thoughtfully? We do; however, it is equally fallible. Much slower than the reactive mindset, it is prone to what psychologists call cognitive overload and depletion, and when that happens it simply gives back control to the reactive mindset. As stated earlier, the exponential increase of information is now at a point where almost all of the information available in the world was created in this century. The capacity for attention – in oneself and in the people we work with – is already becoming an important leadership resource. Attention-deficit is not just a problem in teenagers; it is a serious problem we notice in so many senior managers. It creates emotional exhaustion that we are often unconscious of and we start depleting our cognitive capacities to a point where we fall back into the reactive trap.

The Right Thing to Do

Right action, the defining characteristic of good leadership, requires an entirely different mindset. It begins with the purpose question, 'why do we exist?' This question becomes the guide to acting mindfully from a brain that is evolutionarily prone to either react or procrastinate.

Once we learn to operate from such a mindful mindset we can get to a vision which defines what success would look like at some point in the future. And only after that do we get to strategy. Without purpose, strategy is blind and meaningless. For leaders to operate effectively in a complex, uncertain world, they have to become merchants of meaning, fluent in navigating this complex system.

Right action emerges out of a state of mind that is free from the trap of quick rewards that typically afflict the 'wrong' mindsets that we outlined earlier. Leaders who operate in a mindful mindset have a profoundly clear understanding of the way complex systems work and they are comfortable with the ambiguity of not knowing all the answers. They are more present and curious. They know that the complexities in a situation are highly differentiated, but they are held together by a principle of integration. This integrating principle is simple, but it is usually obscured because it exists at a higher level of cognitive understanding. Rather than waste energy and resources in trying to control the differentiation, they are able to focus their attention on the integrating principle.

In such a state, leaders are able to perceive the issue from a wider, systems perspective in which they are able to do the following:

a) They are fluent with emergent reality and have the ability to adapt quickly to the weak signals emerging from the periphery

b) They are able to quickly get out of the reactive loop of fixed thinking and get into higher order possibilities of creative thinking

c) They utilize feedback from the emergent systems and work with that feedback to create novel opportunities

d) They can tolerate uncertainty and ambiguity for long lengths of time
e) They engage in conversations to discover solutions using multiple perspectives
f) They are able to take a stand in the absence of complete information

Viktor Frankl, Austrian psychologist and a Holocaust survivor, once said, "Ever more people today have the means to live, but no meaning to live for."[17] Enabling others to discover meaning, especially in a complex, uncertain environment is becoming the primary job of leaders. When people begin to operate from a place of meaning, they are automatically drawn to a more productive mindset in which they understand themselves, their roles and the work they do as part of a bigger, more meaningful system. Especially in the complex work environments of the 21st century workplace, such a perspective of life and work is an invaluable resource.

CHAPTER 2

Purpose, Empathy and Meaning

"This is the true joy in life, the being used for a purpose recognized by yourself as a mighty one ... the being a force of nature instead of a feverish selfish little clod of ailments and grievances complaining that the world will not devote itself to making you happy."

GEORGE BERNARD SHAW

Why Rehumanize Leadership?

We were running a workshop for a large European insurance company at a hotel in downtown Shanghai. We had about 30 senior managers in the room. The first day had been about strategy, the second day about finance, and on the third day we began talking about leadership, especially what it took to lead in the increasingly complex context of the 21st century. That afternoon, the conversation turned to the question of awareness and why it played such a critical role in leadership as well as in navigating complexity. We then began exploring the power of purpose, both organizational as well as individual, and why leaders needed to have an answer to why their organization existed. Invariably the conversation meandered to what purpose meant to

the insurance executives, and one or two of the more extra-
verted ones present began to speak about their purpose.

The silences were long and many as the same executives
who had been fluent and articulate in matters of finance and
strategy were now navigating the deeper waters of something much more intractable. The group was largely white
and male, with one person of colour and three women.
Ben was the African-American sitting quietly at one of
the tables, but we had noticed that he was struggling with
his silence, as though he wanted to speak but wasn't able
to find the words to describe what he was going through.
Meanwhile, the conversation on purpose had turned to the
topic of trust. Sensing that something deep and powerful
was going on inside Ben's mind, one of us turned to Ben
and asked him what he felt about all this. That was when
the lid came off and Ben began to speak. In a voice laden
with emotion and holding back his tears, he spoke about
what it meant to be the odd one out in a largely white European insurance company. He talked of his son who, while
looking at the end-of-the-year company magazine that had
photographs of all the senior executives, had asked Ben why
he was the only one who looked different. He spoke of how,
in all the years of working in this firm, he had never had
a meaningful conversation with anyone else about issues
of belonging or the lack of it. By now, the other Americans
in the group were positively squirming in their seats as the
discomfort levels were rising.

Finally, Ben spoke about how this had affected him to
a point he had never felt he was doing meaningful work in
the company. He was merely a shell, he said, and he had
long mastered the ability to turn up at work without really
bringing his human side in. For all these years, he added, he
had sought purpose from outside his work. A long silence

followed and the only sound in the room was that of the air-conditioner whirring away in the Shanghai summer.

Then a strange thing happened: another person got up and began to speak about how he had never disclosed his sexuality openly for the same reasons that Ben gave. He spoke of what it meant to hold back a big part of who he was for fear of being misunderstood. More silence followed. And then one of the women began to speak about what purpose meant for her and how she, too, had never really been able to speak about feeling disenfranchised as a woman in a male-dominated industry and company. Three hours had passed and for the first time these senior insurance executives had engaged in a humanizing conversation about purpose, empathy and meaningful work.

The topic was meant to be about leading in complexity and why purpose mattered. What we had discovered was that once you began probing into these questions they opened up profound questions about identity, trust, community and what ultimately makes us relevant and significant. At about 5pm, we abandoned the formal schedule, brought in a large ice bucket with beers and sat in a circle experiencing a powerful connectivity that had emerged out of nowhere.

For us as leadership educators, the afternoon had been one of immense learning and importance. We had perceived at first-hand how, despite our best efforts, our work places can be unintentionally dehumanizing. In so doing, we undermine the very output we want from our people: high performance, collaboration and great leadership. What's more, no one person is seemingly responsible for suppressing this authentic humanity. Some other powerful, emergent force is at play. How easily our organizations can fall into the trap of ignoring the very aspects of what it means to be human and treat leadership as an instrument for maximizing productivity removed from the very human context that makes productivity possible.

Much work needs to be done to build human-centred leadership that engages with and brings out the best in people. For that, we have to figure out what comes in the way in the form of mindsets, practices and habits and find ways of rehumanizing leadership.

The Absence of Empathy

Ben's outburst came from experiencing a broken story; one that had got unmoored from its source, and that was not leading anywhere. Feeling excluded and devoid of belonging, Ben was experiencing an empathy-deficit from the very organization he wanted to belong to. Empathy fulfills the need for belonging, a deep and unconscious evolutionary need that continues to course through our neural networks as a powerful motivator and driver of behaviour.

For too long have we held the belief that functions of thinking, planning and executing strategies belong to the 'rational brain', a term that is actually an oxymoron. Remember Spock from the original *Star Trek*? Spock, being only half-human, was able to think without any emotion and therefore became the go-to person for Captain Kirk when he had to take a decision that challenged his own frail sense of human morality. Well, Spock doesn't exist despite the fact that so many leaders continue to fantasize about a Spock-like workplace devoid of emotions.

The fact is, emotions are integral to thinking and decision-making and the human brain is incapable of functioning effectively without emotion. The only group that is exempt from this caveat is the psychopaths! One of the more exciting scientific discoveries in recent times is the connection between emotions and the way the brain processes information. Research shows that there is an ongoing conversation between emotions and cognitive processes, with emotions continually regulating the state of the brain. There are more than 40,000 neurons that are working overtime to help our emotions perform this complex function of influencing the brain-state.

While research is continuing on this extraordinary partnership between heart and brain, one thing is eminently clear. Anxiety, feelings of not belonging and a sense of dislocation directly activate the primitive regions of the brain that result in fight-or-flight responses. On the other hand, positive feelings generate activity in the frontal lobes of the brain and are responsible not just for clarity of thinking, but the ability to solve complex problems. The one emotion that does this job better than any other? Empathy.

But empathy is not just about fostering a sense of belonging. Its impact goes far beyond that. In fact, it is arguably one of the top capabilities in a disruptive 21st century. Jeremy Rifkin, in his new book *The Empathic Civilization*,[18] presents a new and insightful interpretation of human civilization. According to Rifkin, not only has the empathic function shaped our development as a species, it is poised to become the critical factor that will decide our fate as a species.

The biological and cognitive sciences are shaping a very different view of human nature than the one that we have adopted for the past several centuries. Recent discoveries in brain science and child development are forcing us to rethink the long-held belief that human beings are, by nature, aggressive, materialistic, utilitarian and self-maximizing. The alternative, that we are a fundamentally empathic species, has profound consequences for the way we lead our organizations and societies.

Empathy in the 21ˢᵗ century

In the book *The Social Leader*, the authors describe three factors that are driving change in the 21ˢᵗ century: "socially created information, global networked communities and the birth of the prosumer". Together, these factors are leading to an increasing blurring of lines between public and private spaces with the creation of a new empathic 'social space'. An increasing number of organizations that were able to function profitably without having to invest more than a rudimentary amount of time, energy and resources into its external relationships are now being pressured to enter that social space.

One such example is PatientsLikeMe (PLM), a for-profit patient network and real-time research platform. PLM helps patients build a network with others who have a similar condition and provides a forum for sharing their experiences. As a result, they are able to contribute data about what is now referred to as the real-world nature of the ailment. The organization has over 600,000 members and its patient-generated data has led to more than 100 peer-reviewed scientific studies. In 2007, PLM was named as one of the '15 Companies that Will Change the World' by *Business 2.0* and *CNN Money*. Co-founders Jamie and Ben Heywood were awarded the 2016 Humanitarian Award by the International Alliance of ALS/MND Associations and, in 2017, PLM was named as one of the Top 10 Most Innovative Companies in Biotech by *Fast Company*.

In a world where patient experience is tightly controlled by the medical industry, this is an example of a social space that is created continually and is communally accessible to all with technology. Most importantly, it has been able to enforce transparency about who uses the data. The twist to the tale is that its partners now include most of the large pharmaceutical companies worldwide, including two of our clients at Duke CE, Sanofi and Novartis. Companies like Sanofi and Novartis have realized that in the 21st century, they are under scrutiny from employees, stakeholders and customers who possess three resources on a scale that is unprecedented: "ubiquitous access to social information, an expectation that they can engage anyone and everyone in conversation to shape the point of view of the community, and the speed of cheap communication that is allowing them to react to events in near real time".[19]

Organizations that were once able to operate autonomously are realizing that their customers are now part of global, networked communities that are driven by passion and purpose. With information becoming a commodity, it is the social relevance of information that becomes a source of advantage. But the problem with social relevance is that it is outside of our jurisdiction of control. Rather, it is the social networks and communities whose actions, decisions and interactions bestow relevance on information. Empathy provides an effective pathway for operating effectively in this landscape. Moreover, a new millennial demographic has the mindset of the 'prosumer', with the ability to use technology and armed with a mindset of transparency, participation and engagement rather than one of receiving information. Employees, consumers and stakeholders "expect to have a voice in the products and strategy of companies they care about".[20]

Meaning-Makers and Story-Tellers

We are unique as a species in that we are driven by an innate and compelling desire to find meaning in our lives and in the work that we do. And once we do find that meaning, we function better as creative human beings; we feel more complete, we are more productive and we experience greater wellbeing. But meaning is arrived at obliquely, much like wellbeing. This means that it is a by-product rather than a means to something. Chasing meaning is a futile process as it doesn't have any existence in itself; rather we find meaning when we are being of service or, as positive psychologist Martin Seligman puts it, "… using your signature strengths and virtues in the service of something much larger than you are".[21]

To contribute, to be of use and to be of service triggers a sense of wellbeing in our brains that is very different from the experience of fleeting pleasure. The yearning for the 'why' is a universal need, and the need to find answers to the ultimate questions of life seems to be hardwired into our brains. From the ancient Greeks, who differentiated the logical from the teleological, to the Buddhist view of 'dharma', meaning has occupied a central position in human thought over the centuries. Meaning provides perspective and instills in us a sense of 'deep time', which is very different from the sense of rushed time that has become such a common affliction.

Not only are we meaning-makers, we are also consummate story-tellers. We live our lives through a narrative that has been put together by us and others. In the book *The Stories We Are*,[22] author William Randall plays with the possibility that we each make sense of the events of our lives to the extent that we weave them into our own unfolding novel as, simultaneously, its author, narrator, main character and reader. "The Universe is made of stories, not of atoms," wrote Muriel Rukeyser,[23] emphasizing how we can only make sense of who we are and how we became who we are through how we make meaning of our experiences. And if those stories are purposeful stories, the narrative is that much more powerful, enduring and energizing. The stories we are and the stories we tell ourselves and others literally help us create ourselves.

Studies such as the 'Midlife in the United States Study' (MIDUS) have reported that those with a significant purpose in their lives were far more likely to outlive their peers. There is a branch of therapy called 'Narrative Therapy', which is all about assisting people to create stories about themselves, about their identities, that are helpful to them. This work of 're-authoring identity' helps people identify their own values and articulate the skills and knowledge they have to live these values. Through the process of helping people rewrite their stories, narrative therapy brings meaning back into people's lives.

New research in neurology also points out that we can make deep changes in our reality by making changes in the language and the linguistic concepts we use to understand and describe the world around us. Using purpose-centred concepts allows leaders to shape a reality in which people feel a sense of belonging and purpose. These are powerful humanizing tools that produce amplifying effects. Organizations play a vital role in meaning-making by providing the space for their people to engage in meaningful work.

The Purpose of Purpose

'Just do it' might be a great motivating line from a shoemaker, but in the absence of purpose it is the hardest thing to do. We cannot just do: we want to know why we must and why we can't. And therein lies the ultimate conundrum of the ages: to do what one must do, one must know what one is to do. But to do it well we need to know why we must do it.

Can we assume that life has a purpose? That the events that punctuate our life are all part of some grand design? From Aristotle's unmoved mover to the attempts by various religions to convey their interpretations of what that design could be, the history of civilization has seen many attempts to convey the notion of a purposeful universe. But equally, there have been compelling theories from the other side of the fence that demonstrate the utter randomness of life. The simple answer to the question of whether life has a purpose is that we simply do not know and, perhaps, we may never know. But there is a far more important question. Despite the distinct possibility that we may well be existing in a random universe, do we need to have purpose in order to live well or to perform well in whatever we are doing? The answer to this question is a resounding yes. To paraphrase the much-quoted saying, the purpose of life may well be to live a life with purpose.

From a neurological perspective, the question 'why' emerges out of brain activity in the orbito-frontal region of the brain, the region that is responsible for reflection and thinking. The need to know why separates us from most of the other life forms on the planet. But, to want purpose is at once a gift of evolution as well as a burden. As far as we know, we are the only species on the planet that has the ability to think succinctly of a future or a past state and ascribe meaning to it while being in the present. This is one of the big leaps in the development of the human brain, but it also comes at a huge emotional cost. That is because the question why is not just any question, it is richly imbued with the quest for fulfillment and meaning and the joy of discovering it. But equally well, it can be accompanied by the pain of not finding it. It's very presence and articulation can become a rallying call for thousands of people in an organization or in a society, but equally well its absence can be a reflection of the dark night of the soul and that phase of meaninglessness that so many of us go through. The legend of Sisyphus, who was doomed to keep carrying a boulder up the mountain only to see it roll down again, describes the deep mythical dread of a life without meaning.

Is the work that we do worth doing? And why do we do it? G.H. Hardy, the great English mathematician raised this question in his monumental 1940 book, *A Mathematician's Apology*.[24] Hardy was only paraphrasing the question that has plagued humankind for millennia: why are we here? 'Purpose': just the word draws us into a sense of the beginning of things, the source from which everything must emerge. It is also connected with a deep sense of wellbeing, of lives well lived and that inevitable sense of contentment we must find when we find our purpose.

And it is curious how we use the terms 'finding' or 'discovering' to prefix purpose, which prompts the question of when and how exactly do we lose our purpose that we have to find it or discover it? More importantly, how do we regain it? Also, when we refer to a 'sense of purpose', we convey that purpose is derived not from rational reasoning but more from a process of sense-making. The reason this is important is that we cannot approach purpose through the same lens as strategy. Later in this book, we will refer to 'excavating purpose' to describe that process. Buried deep under, we have to find ways of allowing it to surface.

Purpose is the life-force that runs through us and our organizations. The words we use to describe its presence are words like direction, passion, wellbeing, productivity, clarity, engagement and even joy. Organizations with a sense of purpose that goes beyond shareholder value are more productive and innovative. Purpose-led brands sell more. Employees and associates who have a deeper sense of purpose are more engaged and creative. Purpose-centred leaders are more likely to build high-performing teams and lead sustainable enterprises. They leave behind a legacy.

Rehumanizing Leadership for the 21st Century: Purpose, Empathy and Meaning

The process of rehumanizing leadership is about consciously positioning the organization at the intersection of purpose, empathy and meaning.

Purpose provides the living reason why we exist in the first place and channels that reason into every aspect of your organization. Purpose provides direction and clarity and it motivates us to do the right thing but, more importantly, from a 21st century perspective it provides the channels for remaining adaptable and relevant in a rapidly dislocating world. It does that by guiding us to play our part in the larger ecosystem by building relationships of trust and value. Purpose allows strategy to stay agile and nimble and it is instrumental in helping the organization to navigate through ambiguity and focusing its attention on what is important.

Purpose provides the 'why', the reason why we exist as an organization and it addresses three fundamental questions:

Why do we exist?
What is the unique contribution we want to make?
How do we make the world a better place by being here?

We shall be spending more time on the process of crafting purpose later in the book, but what we want to stress right away is that purpose predates strategy. We quoted Dave Packard in the previous chapter. This is the full quote of the statement he made in 1960 and it is still as relevant today, if not even more so:

I want to discuss why a company exists in the first place. In other words, why are we here? I think many people assume, wrongly, that a company exists simply to make money. While this is an important result of a company's existence, we have to go deeper to find the real reasons for our being ... as we investigate this, we inevitably come to the conclusion that a group of people get together and exist as an institution that we call a company so they are able to accomplish something collectively that they could not accomplish separately–they **make a contribution to society, a phrase which sounds trite but is fundamental ...**

Empathy, in the way we use the word, is much more than just emotional empathy as in being able to put oneself in another's shoes. The journey to empathy is arduous and deeply humanizing as it is the result of dropping self-importance and the delusion of past knowledge. And purpose, because it is anchored in service, lifts our gaze above pure ego and thus enables greater empathy. Empathy is the medium through which we build trust and a community, both internally and externally. From a 21st century perspective, empathy becomes the inescapable force for designing our place in the ecosystem. Empathic organizations build value in our ecosystems and our networks.

Meaning is the ultimate lifeblood of any human endeavour. Human beings are meaning-makers as the need to contribute to a larger story is endemic to our evolution as a species. When we work within complex systems that are an indelible part of the 21st century landscape, meaning-generation becomes a critical necessity as that creates relevance. Meaning provides the organization and its members with the answer to one fundamental question: how do we stay relevant in a fast-changing world?

Rehumanizing leadership in our organizations is about engaging in three key tasks: one, excavating the organization's purpose and helping members of the organization to connect deeply with that; two, engendering the higher psychological driver of empathy in its members; and three, creating the space for meaningful work that allows the members of the organization to experience relevance and significance.

Human Resources to Human Beings

For this we will have to disband the belief that employees are resources to be utilized for the benefit of the corporation. We will also have to disband the belief that customers and consumers are passive recipients of our products and services. When we flip these beliefs around and begin positioning people, be they your employees or your customers, as participants in the process of rehumanization, it transforms the relationship you and your organization has with them.

It must be mentioned at the outset that humanizing leadership is not a new idea at all. But the 20th century saw a gradual shift away from the humanized workplace, despite attempts by humanistic thinkers such as Mary Parker Follett, Abraham Maslow and Peter Drucker among many others. Bureaucratic hierarchies became the order of the day and, especially from the eighties onwards, maximizing shareholder value became the tune that needed to be danced to. Large public organizations that did not have shareholders simply became more bureaucratic.

Stephen Denning, writing in a post in the 7th Global Drucker Forum writes about the unholy alliance between shareholder value and hierarchical bureaucracy:[25]

Once a firm embraces maximizing shareholder value and the current stock price as its goal, and lavishly compensates top management to that end, the C-suite has little choice but to deploy command-and-control management. That's because making money for shareholders and the C-suite is inherently uninspiring to employees. The C-suite must compel employees to obey. The result is that only one in five employees is fully engaged in his or her work, and even fewer are passionate. The very foundations of humanist management – collaboration and trust – are missing.

Why always precedes How

Our contention is that the 21st century is systematically dismantling the world as we once knew it. A new order that is emerging out of digital technology and global information flows is forcing change on the 20th century organizational form. The big transformation has already begun. Information has become a commodity and assets have given way to access. Digital software is eating away at the 20th century edifices and they are starting to crumble faster than we can manage. Aided by technology and information, customers are increasingly in control. Employees, once at the mercy of the rich and powerful owners, and later the C-suite, are suddenly participants in the organization's story. As Denning writes, "But the most important battle in the war for humanistic management – compelling firms to respect customers and employees as human beings – has already been won. The choice for organizations today is: change or die."[26]

For us, the imperative to rehumanize leadership has never been greater. In fact, we feel that it has become one of the most pressing issues of our time. Two of our biggest clients, a leading pharmaceutical company and a successful global bank, have both been on a journey of over two years in doing precisely this, with very tangible rewards.

In recent years, Simon Sinek's TED Talk on what he referred to as the 'golden circle' and putting 'why' at the centre of it unleashed a new interest in this topic.[27] Purpose is re-entering the vocabulary of the 21st century workplace. The last three decades saw strategy become the Holy Grail for businesses and organizations. Strategy is fine as long as the world in which one is operating is stable and reasonably predictable. Take that away and your strategy is as good as its last iteration.

As the pace of life has accelerated and the world become more uncertain, the purpose of a company has a key role in helping its leaders navigate through the chaos. But purpose is not just that feel-good rallying call; it takes hard work to institutionalize purpose, as Denise Pickett, President of American Express' US consumer service division empha- sized when we interviewed her: "Purpose won't work unless it's 'institutionalized' – everyone from the guy in the post room to the Chief Executive must buy into it and live it."

We are constantly working with companies whose main focus is about getting the strategy right and Pickett's con- trasting of strategy and purpose is very incisive:

Strategy is always chunked down and changed to target different levels of the business ... it will never be digestible for everyone all together – so it cannot be a guiding light for 10,000 people. Purpose is a long-term investment, and that's where you get the alignment with shareholder interest. The outcome is better for shareholders, but it's not the starting point or rallying point. Sharehold- ers are not the guiding light. If you put the employee engagement first, and then keep customers at the centre, shareholder returns will follow.

Perhaps that is Pickett's greatest insight: if you lead your people from a clear sense of purpose, profits will naturally follow.

We will be building on Pickett's insights and showing you how the so-called golden circle of the 'why' actually emerges out of a framework of constraints. We will then use this framework to help you build and institutionalize purpose in your organization.

We will show you how some of the leaders we have worked with are able to rehumanize leadership through purpose, empathy and the creation of meaning. This is what this book is all about. But let us start at the beginning. We are going to do this by examining the most important assumptions we have been making all through the 20th century, about our organizations, work and leadership. We want to show you how these assumptions came out of social narratives that we interpreted as being the truth. It is only then that we can start building new narratives that are relevant for the 21st century.

CHAPTER 3

New Principles for the 21st Century

"You never change things by fighting the existing reality. To change something, build a new model that makes the existing model obsolete."

BUCKMINSTER FULLER

When one of our research associates typed in the term 'rehumanizing leadership' into her search, the algorithm immediately suggested an alternative: 'dehumanizing leadership'. That just about sums up the reason for writing this book, just in case we needed that reassurance! Another email caught our attention recently, one from *Harvard Business Review* that read "How to be human at work?" Then *Forbes* topped that with an article that read, "Five ways to be more human at work". No wonder dehumanizing leadership comes up as default for rehumanizing leadership in internet searches!

We place our work, *Rehumanizing Leadership*, squarely in the context of the 21st century, a term we will use right through the book to describe the emerging global landscape in which our organizations are being disrupted and dislocated from the familiar past. What is happening is that a dominant social narrative that has been responsible for shaping our worldview, our beliefs and our choices is coming to the end of its tether. This is the narrative that claims that human beings are fundamentally selfish and work primarily for self-maximization and that self-interest at the expense of others is what constitutes human nature. Social narratives are like stories that shape our behaviour and, in turn, our shaped behaviour ends up reinforcing the storyline thereby getting us into a vicious tangle of self-fulfilling prophecies. Once we adopt such a narrative, it becomes easy to rational-ize structures that promote self-maximization.

But if we had an alternative narrative, like the philosophy of Ubuntu from the African continent, an idea that roughly translates as 'I am because you are', it changes the way in which we think of ourselves and of the work that we do. We are not denying that self-interest is not real. However, it is putting self-interest above all else that ultimately leads us to build social structures that promote exactly that.

To better understand this, we need to dig deeper into the three supportive beliefs that have been responsible for holding up the self-maximizing narrative.

1. The belief that we are separate from nature

The belief that we are separate from nature is a powerful assumption that has prevailed for centuries. It was played out in the early days of the pioneers and colonizers for whom nature was something to be tamed. Early accounts of Aboriginal people in the Americas and Australasia reveal their disbelief and horror at the way the early colonizers viewed nature as an enemy, as it went completely against how they perceived their relationship with nature. As we shall see later in Chapter 4, it was only in the sixties that the first account of the consequences of this assumption began to emerge and we began to understand the complex systems in nature and what ecosystems are all about.

2. The belief that thoughts and emotions are two separate things

This narrative emerges in the writings of early European philosophers such as René Descartes, for whom the human being was conceived in terms of a mind inhabiting a body. The mind (*res cogitans*) was perceived to be infinitely superior to the body (*res extensa*) and so was responsible for controlling the body – which includes emotions – which were seen as an unnecessary encumbrance. The assumption that thoughts control emotions is a powerful myth that continues to this day. Sadly, it also feeds into a parallel and misguided narrative of equating rational thought as masculine and emotion as feminine. We now have clear, scientific evidence that shows how thinking necessarily involves emotions, whether you are a man or a woman. Also, new research in medicine has given us far more awareness of the intricate connections between the mind and the body and the psychosomatic origins of many a 'dis-ease'.

3. The notion of the universe as machine

Clockmaking was the most sophisticated industry in 17th century Europe and the image of a gigantic clock ticking away became the defining metaphor for the universe. It served two important requirements. First, having clear, understandable 'laws of nature' satisfied the requirement of deterministic science of the time – science that was based principally on the twin assumptions of certainty and predictability. Second, it served to satisfy the religious clergy by positioning God as the ultimate clockmaker who wound the clock for it to tick away until eternity. Through this worldview, physics became the search for understanding how this 'perfect' clock worked and for uncovering the rules that governed its functioning. The machine metaphor of the universe soon became the template for the way we designed societies and organizations. Machines provided a convenient way of designing for control and predictability in the industrial age.

Survival of the Fittest

It was with Darwin's theory of evolution that the self-maximizing narrative reached its crescendo, conditioning future generations to blindly subscribe to the 'survival of the fittest' ideology. Interestingly, as an aside, Darwin never used this phrase and we will never know what exactly Herbert Spencer meant by it. In fact, Darwin wrote in *The Descent of Man*,[28] "Those communities which included the greatest number of the most sympathetic members would flourish best and rear the greatest number of offspring." Darwin called it the "almost ever-present instinct".

Notwithstanding what Darwin called it, the march of the self-maximizing doctrine continued well into the 20ᵗʰ century. Severing our ties with nature, identifying ourselves as independent atomic units with a machine-like perception of the universe led us down a fragmented, mechanistic worldview in which self-interest overrode every other concern. Assuming the narrative to be real, we built social structures based on these assumptions, leading to a slow and steady dehumanizing process. By then, the belief that managers represented the mind of the organization and workers the body had given credence to the need to control, monitor and coordinate as the number one role of the manager. An interesting architectural spin-off of this way of thinking was the emergence of the mezzanine floor in factories where managers could stand and 'supervise' the workers on the shop floor. Naturally, incentives were based on the carrot and stick approach and that allowed the feudal nature of management to continue.

In the centuries that followed, the mechanistic model composed of elementary building blocks began to shape the human perception of organizations. This led to mechanistic theories of management with the aim of increasing efficiency by designing organizations in the same interlocking way; departments and functions linked by clear lines of control and communication. As manufacturing became the dominant industry, the machine became a very convenient metaphor. Morgan, in his classic work *Images of Organizations,*[29] wrote, "Organizations that used machines became more and more like machines."

Enter the Shareholders

It was in the early 20th century that management as a pseudo-science made its presence felt. Management theorists like Frederick Taylor (1911) built on the machine metaphor and designed principles that would have organizations run with machine-like efficiency. Bureaucracy was equally important as it helped to run the organizations with precision. As Morgan points out: "Work is often organized in the minutest detail on the basis of designs that analyze the total process of production, find the most efficient procedures and then allocate these as specialized duties to people trained to perform in a very precise way. All the thinking is done by the managers and designers, leaving all the doing to the employees."[30]

Fast-forward to the seventies when Milton Friedman's view of economics and maximizing profits for shareholders at the expense of everything else became the mantra for business. With Friedman's work, the self-maximizing narrative crystallized into a doctrine that would continue to dominate business thinking to this day.

It happened through an article published in the *New York Times* magazine in 1970, denouncing corporate 'social responsibility' as a 'socialist doctrine'. The assertion that Friedman made was that "the manager is the agent of the individuals who own the corporation". Going further, he wrote, the manager's primary "responsibility is to conduct the business in accordance with [the owners'] desires." The executive was described as "an agent serving the interests of his principal". In 1976, the *Journal of Financial Economics* carried a seminal paper called 'Theory of the Firm'.[31] Harvard Business School professors Joseph Bower and Lynn Paine spelled out what the Theory of the Firm was all about in a 2017 *Harvard Business Review* article titled 'The Error at the Heart of Corporate Leadership':[32]

- *Shareholders own the corporation and are 'principals' with original authority to manage the corporation's business and affairs*
- *Managers are delegated decision-making authority by the corporation's shareholders and are thus 'agents' of the shareholders*
- *As agents of the shareholders, managers are obliged to conduct the corporation's business in accordance with shareholders' desires*
- *Shareholders want business to be conducted in a way that maximizes their own economic returns*

Theory of the Firm is packed with research, statistical models and plenty of complicated graphs. The field was to become known as mathematical economics, with applications to social problems. Wall Street loved the theory and the die had been cast. Short-termism was here to stay, with far reaching repercussions for the management of organizations and for society as a whole.

This is not to say that there were no exceptions; there was Jamsetji Tata in India, William Lever in England and many others with the belief that the business had a much bigger role in society than purely selfish gains. But these were exceptions and the dominant narrative remained the same, profit at the expense of everything else. That is why philanthropy, which later became corporate and social responsibility, meant well, but it did not intend to challenge the dominant worldview of self-maximization. This is reflected in Kopernik's experience with large corporations. As their Chief Operating Officer, Ewa Wojkowska states, "CSR can sometimes get in the way of innovation and change because it's usually an add-on and not integrated with the core business of the company. So, its ability to fundamentally change thinking is limited."

What is the role of business in the 21st century?

An important 2018 study titled 'Leaders on Purpose'[33] studied 16 global CEOs in order to develop insight on purpose-driven leadership. The researchers had some stringent criteria for the choice of the CEOs: they had to have operations in multiple countries; they had to have financial metrics within the top sector quartile; they had to have a commitment to sustainability and/or to purpose; and they had to have a sustainability ranking of being in the top 50% of environment, social and governance rankings. The CEOs who were interviewed shared many valuable insights, but did not have all the answers. Fortunately, they are asking the right questions: how do we balance the quest for profits with responsible growth? Is it possible to do good and do well? What is the future of business leadership?

The seven most pressing external challenges for the CEOs in their study were:

1. *Climate Change*
2. *Malnutrition*
3. *Wealth disparity*
4. *Migration*
5. *Short-termism*
6. *Declining trust in institutions*
7. *Employment and technology*

Looking at this list, these CEOs are observing a world far more complex and interdependent and at a scale that is unlike anything we have known so far. From a 20th century perspective, these factors would be seen as external to the purview of business. No longer. As the 'Leaders on Purpose' paper asks, "What is the role of business in society today? For a long time, the notions of social responsibility and profit were decoupled. Today, we recognize that business is a critical lever in addressing the global challenges of an increasingly complex and interconnected world. Through investments, new business models and innovative products and services, the role and impact of organizations is constantly and rapidly changing." One of the CEOs in the study went far enough to say, "The reason why we exist is because we are adding to the communities where we live ..."

Everyone Better Off

We met Jayne-Anne Gadhia when she was the CEO of Virgin Money to ask her the same question. She wrote her book, *The Virgin Banker*,[34] in 2017. Jayne-Anne is emphatic that the success of Virgin Money is due to a powerful sense of purpose. This is what she said when we began the conversation on purpose: "In the aftermath of the financial crisis, public trust in banks and bankers was broken. With empires built on sand, bankers appeared to be part of an untouchable (male-only) club, motivated by fat-cat pay packets and the adrenaline of the next big deal. There appeared to be little regard of the responsibility and privilege that comes from employing hardworking people serving customers. The firmer foundations of social responsibility were ultimately dismissed in the win-at-all-cost pursuit of growth and glory. I saw at first-hand what the pursuit of profit, to the detriment of everything else, can do to the long-term health of a business."

Jayne-Anne returned to head up Virgin Money in 2007, with the determination to lead a business with a strong sense of purpose. "Yes, we wanted to make profit for our shareholders. But absolutely not at the expense of everything else. We wanted our communities to flourish!" Along with her team, they came to a resolution that "our ambition and central purpose would be to make everyone better off". Make everyone better off (EBO) became a rallying cry for purpose and values at Virgin Money. "Making our EBO ethos, ambition and intent explicit, almost as a call to arms, ensured buy-in from colleagues. It galvanized people within the business and I am certain that is the reason Virgin Money has been so successful."

Purpose and Profit

As the paper by 'Leaders on Purpose' demonstrates, Jayne-Anne at Virgin Money makes a strong case for the logic that companies that can demonstrate a strong purpose are more successful. Moreover, today's generation wants transparent, genuine leadership and they are far more exacting in their expectations of their employers than before. We asked Jayne-Anne about how the purpose of EBO had motivated her and colleagues at Virgin Money, especially those from a younger demographic. Jayne-Anne replied that what they did at Virgin Money was nothing short of building a movement. "We wanted to create a movement of people that not only wanted banking to be better, but that wanted to make a positive contribution to society." Virgin Money EBO made a commitment to the government: "No redundancies, no branch closures, maintaining our operational headquarters in Newcastle and much more besides that". Pausing for a few seconds, Jayne-Anne continued; "That meant we were able to buy Northern Rock, operate it with purpose and return the business to profitability."

A key strategy that Virgin Money followed was to put EBO at the heart of the business. This is just what Unilever had done with their Unilever Sustainable Living Plan (USLP) in 2007. For Virgin Money, this meant that EBO was part of everyday decision-making, resulting in strong outcomes for everyone in the organization "because purpose and the desire to make a real difference is what gets people out of bed in the morning: not spreadsheets and models!" In true Virgin fashion, EBO became the inspiring force for a new venture called 'Virgin Money Giving'. This led to working with a huge range of charities and good causes. Since its launch in 2009, the company has donated over £660 million to charities through Virgin Money Group. This has resulted in over £20 million more reaching charities because the team chose to operate it as a not-for-profit service. It was also the EBO thinking that led to the creation of the Virgin Money lounges. Jayne-Anne told us why customers love the lounges: they don't look like banks and they don't behave like banks. Jayne-Anne has always believed that caring for the community that you serve has to be at the heart of the business. It cannot be assigned to a function or a department. "Some big organizations have a Corporate Social Responsibility department. A nice thing to have to make a CEO feel good about themselves," said Jayne-Anne without hiding the way she feels about the topic. "To me, social responsibility is not a departmental issue. It is a business issue. And that's why we made EBO part of the fabric, energy, conversations and culture – the beating heart of Virgin Money."

Jayne-Anne still doesn't fit into the image of the city banker and the 'old-boy network' that she writes about in the concluding chapter of her book. To the question, "Why did no one see the crisis coming?" she writes, "Some did. In my opinion they just chose to do nothing about it, for fear of saying the wrong thing or being excluded from the network." Diversity is the only way to break this stranglehold of male-dominated bastions, according to Jayne-Anne. And despite being called 'a difficult woman' to her face, she writes, "In doing business in a new way, and doing it well and with purpose, I have never found any issues in being a woman in banking ..." And, "In the end, I have always felt that if you do what you believe is right, with integrity, you can't go far wrong."

Jayne-Anne's strength of conviction comes from her keen sense of purpose. She adds: "I have found that, whatever life has thrown at me, the best thing always has been to work hard and find my purpose. Everything seems so much worthwhile if you truly believe that your efforts will have some sort of positive and lasting effect on the world around you."

Leadership for
What's Next

We feel that the dominant narrative of self-maximization that we have accepted as truth and which has led it to becoming the pervasive worldview for business is reaching its obsolescence. Organization and business leaders will have to ask themselves the following questions if they are to successfully navigate through the 21st century:

Do you have a sustainable strategy for an environment that is being rapidly disrupted by a combination of factors over which you have no control?

Is your leadership producing the results that you are expecting from a fast-moving 21st century organization?

Does your leadership and the strategy of the organization help to unlock human energy? Do your people think and feel that they are doing meaningful work?

Are your people broadly aligned as well as energized in service of your customers, stakeholders and society?

Do your people feel that they have the degrees of freedom to experiment, invent and rethink?

Is your organization relevant in the larger ecosystem and creating value for it?

If you are struggling with some of the answers, it is time to rehumanize leadership. The self-maximization narrative needs to be replaced by a new narrative of interdependence. Terms such as 'inclusive capitalism' and 'conscious capitalism' have been appearing for a while in CEO roundtables and conversations. There is a greater awareness of ecosystems and interdependencies, not just in the natural environment but in the way we operate. Globalization and digital technology are creating a new mindset about interconnectedness. And digital technology is creating networks of transparency in which we are far more aware of the impact of our choices and the choices of others. Never before has the human race been so interconnected. Digital technology is levelling out the playing field faster than ever before. A taxi driver in Mumbai has access to the same information on social media that you have in New York. Consumers can bring down your sales if they find that your brands are not sustainable. Likewise, brands that demonstrate their sustainability credentials make for greater loyalty. A new 'Reputation Economy' is emerging around us that will test not how successful we are but how relevant we are in the ecosystem. Trust is the new currency and integrity is the new must-have asset for your organization in an increasingly transparent 21st century.

Power Shifts

The two vectors of purpose and empathy are shaping the 21st century landscape faster than we can see. Hierarchical leadership is fading away and it is taking with it all its associated attributes. Ernest J. Wilson III of the University of Southern California calls these new attributes the 'third space', that is distinct from the typical MBA and engineering perspectives that have dominated management thinking for decades. He listed the following critical attributes from his research, in a September 2015 *Harvard Business Review* article:[35] "Adaptability, cultural competence (the capacity to think, act and move across multiple borders),

360-degree thinking (holistic understanding, capable of recognizing patterns of problems and their solutions), intellectual curiosity and, of course, empathy."

In *New Power*,[36] Jeremy Heimans and Henry Timms explore what is going to work in a 'chaotic world' and they point to a shift from old power, which was all about formal governance, resource consolidation, confidentiality and discretion, expertise and specialization, and less overall participation. New power values for the authors are about informal governance, open sourcing, radical transparency, a do-it-yourself ethic and more overall participation.

In their 2015 *Harvard Business Review* article "Understanding New Power",[37] the same authors wrote:

> *Old power works like a currency. It is held by few. Once gained, it is jealously guarded and the powerful have a substantial store of it to spend. It is closed, inaccessible and leader-driven. It downloads and it captures. New power operates differently, like a current. It is made by many. It is open, participatory and peer-driven. It uploads and it distributes. Like water or electricity, it's most forceful when it surges. The goal with new power is not to hoard it but to channel it.*

For us, power in the 21st century is going to be less about entitlement, status and position. It is not so much about how powerful you are, but how you can use power wisely. The two vectors of purpose and empathy provide the methodology and the tools to lead in the 21st century. The rest of the book will explore how we can do this.

Part 2

Why
Change
Is Possible

"Never doubt that a small group
of thoughtful, committed,
citizens can change the world.
Indeed, it is the only thing
that ever has."

MARGARET MEAD

CHAPTER 4

Navigating Complexity in the 21st Century

"When we try to pick out anything by itself, we find it hitched to everything else in the universe."

JOHN MUIR, *Nature Writings*

In 1962, a small, innocuous book went on to ignite the environmental movement and bring about the first awareness of our 'eco-system'. The book was called *Silent Spring*[38] and its author, Rachel Carson, a biologist, began its first chapter, 'A Fable for Tomorrow', with the words: "There was once a town in the heart of America where all life seemed to live in harmony with its surroundings. The town lay in the midst of a checkerboard of prosperous farms, with fields of grain and hillsides of orchards where, in spring, white clouds of bloom drifted above the green fields ..." After a few more lines came these words: "Then a strange blight crept over the area and everything began to change. Some evil spell had settled on the community: mysterious maladies swept the flocks of chickens; the cattle and sheep sickened and died. Everywhere was a shadow of death ... there was a strange stillness."

Carson decided to write *Silent Spring* after receiving a letter from a friend who notified her that the aerial spraying of DDT (dichlorodiphenyltrichloroethane), a pesticide, had devastated a local wildlife sanctuary. Soon after the release of the book, there was a violent reaction from the establishment, which used every possible means to gag her. Accused of being a communist, the unkindest cut of all was from the former Secretary of Agriculture Ezra Taft Benson, who asked, "Why a spinster with no children was so concerned about genetics?"

Carson's dignity and sense of purpose allowed her to withstand the blows from the establishment. At the same time, she was fighting cancer. A doctor's negligence had led to the cancer metastasizing. Then in 1963, President Kennedy heard about *Silent Spring* and he asked for a Congressional hearing to regulate the use of pesticides. Despite the pain in her weakening body, Rachel Carson went on to testify at the hearings. The Science Advisory Committee was able to refute the objections of her critics and the first federal environmental policies to protect the planet came into being. In one of the letters she wrote to her friend, Dorothy Freeman, Carson writes, "This is a book about man's war against nature and, because man is part of nature, it is also inevitably a book about man's war against himself."

Rachel Carson was posthumously awarded the Presidential Medal of Freedom. *Silent Spring* became the heartbeat of the environmental movement and brought about a new consciousness of our relationship with our complex ecosystem. Today, DDT is banned worldwide under the Stockholm Convention in 2001.

Our Discomfort with Complexity

We decided to bring in Rachel Carson's work to start a conversation on how little we really understand complex systems. Long after the book was published in 1962, it took for

Chernobyl to happen in 1986 for us to learn that pollution has no nationality and that the Earth's ecosystem is one vast interconnected network. Life is essentially a complex system; even the simplest living system – a bacterial cell – is a highly complex network involving literally thousands of interdependent chemical reactions. The same goes for the human body.

And the same is true for all social systems. Human organizations are essentially complex systems operating with similar principles that are true of other complex systems. However, up until the 21st century it was relatively easy to ignore complexity as a phenomenon and so we continued to impose linear structures of hierarchy and vertical power on our organizations.

But the forces of digital technology, transparency and equal access to information are weakening the linear structures of hierarchy and power and are unleashing the 'network power' of human interactions. Moreover, new generations are able to resist these old linear structures with more authority, as they are the ones who are controlling the technology. The big challenge is our ability to transform the way we lead our organizations and the way we work if we are to thrive in an increasingly complex 21st century. We carry a heavy legacy of linearity.

Understanding Complex Systems

All through the 20th century, it was convenient to largely disregard complex or non-linear systems. One of us was trained as a physicist and remembers how routinely we converted non-linear complex equations into linear ones by a simple process of approximation. As Fritjof Capra and Pier Luigi Luisi write in *The Systems View of Life*,[39] "Thus instead of describing phenomena in their full complexity, the linear equations of science dealt with small oscillations, shallow waves, small changes of temperature. This habit became so ingrained that many equations were linearized while being set up, so that science textbooks did not even include the non-linear versions!"

The 20th century, in fact, was a love affair with straight lines, which is what linear equations are all about. We were happy as long as we could approximate complex phenomena into linear equations. Linearity allowed us to continue believing in certainty and predictability; as we wrote in Chapter 1, this kept both classical science and the church happy. There is another factor: it seems as if our brains may have a bias towards linearity and the need for quick, understandable explanations. We have a preference for the availability of information – however flawed it is – to deal with the silence of ambiguity. Similarly, we have a preference for automatic biases that provide us with an illusion of knowing rather than the vulnerability of not knowing. And so we tend to fill in the gaps, join the dots and create explanations and theories that allow us to feel we are in control. That is why we tend to opt for the speedy efficiency of linearity. Our linear preference emerges out of ancient survival mechanisms that once kept us alive. The problem is that they are not suited to the complex, interconnected networks of the 21st century.

That is precisely why we do not easily perceive patterns of interconnection; instead, we prefer to see disconnected autonomous entities that can be managed independently. In *Silent Spring* Rachel Carson was looking at a fairly obvious complex system in which synthetic pesticides were having an impact beyond their intended target. While DDT did kill the pests as intended, it had unintended consequences right up the food chain (or more accurately up the food 'web').

Because we do not perceive complex, interdependent systems and, instead, see fragmented structures, our actions are similarly fragmented. That is the reason we are obsessed with structure in our organizations as it is the easiest thing to fix.

It gives us the semblance of change and, at the same time, makes us feel secure in the knowledge that we have a structure! Our performance management systems are based on a similar logic. Elaborate processes of control and an entire internal industry with full-time employees, tons of paperwork and checks and counter-checks help to provide an illusion of activity, but it has absolutely no bearing on improving performance! In fact, the failure of performance management systems is one of the biggest revelations that HR has to deal with right now. Biases serve as a guide to the future because of the familiar past, and they work as long as the future follows a similar trajectory. We resort to linear solutions to address complex problems: the problem is that they do not work.

Complexity is not Complicatedness!

We often mistake complexity for complicatedness and we tend to use the two terms interchangeably. But the two are totally different phenomena. A watch is a complicated piece of machinery. So is the space shuttle. Parts and pieces that work together in complicated ways. But they are not complex systems. On the other hand, traffic at an intersection is a complex phenomenon. So is any human grouping or any organization.

Search for the Choluteca Bridge in Honduras on the internet and you will find an eerie picture of the bridge that abruptly ends at the river rather than going over the river. It is not a photo-shopped picture. The truth is that the US Army built the bridge over the river in 1930, but no one at that time could have predicted that Hurricane Mitch would alter the course of the river in 1998. The bridge serves as an evocative example of complexity and the emergent possibilities that cannot be forecasted and planned. What happened to the Choluteca Bridge was part of a complex system phenomenon.

A complex system is composed of interconnected parts and it exhibits properties that are not obvious from the properties of the individual parts. Think back to the long tradition of reductionism that has dominated Western thought: it is essentially about understanding parts and assuming that we therefore understand the whole. While reductionism and subsequent analysis gives us detail, it fails to give us perspective. Dissecting a flower stem and observing its parts under a microscope may give us an understanding of the xylem, phloem and the vascular bundles, but it doesn't provide us with the relationship the stem has with the rest of the ecosystem. The functions and departments in the structure of your organization provide a semblance of order and control, but they do not help in building networks with the external ecosystem.

Both perspectives – the fragmentary and the interdependent – are important and necessary. However, while focusing on the parts became the dominant methodology of science and later on went on to influence sociology, economics and management, we lost sight of the whole and we lost the ability to understand the relationship between the two. We struggle even today.

This is the reason why complexity challenges our traditional fragmentary worldview in which we tend to focus on parts, rather than the whole. Complexity is not a new phenomenon; in fact, it is as old as life itself: the most fundamental principle of life.

Take a leaf for example. Does the leaf end at its contours? Yes, from a linear perspective, but no from a complex, interdependent perspective. What the latter says is that the leaf, in fact, begins at its contours as that is where it enters into a relationship with the rest of the ecosystem. Incidentally, the ecosystem includes the sun that fixes the chlorophyll that is necessary for the sustenance of life on the planet. The network of interdependencies and interconnections is necessarily a complex system in that it is dynamic, self-regulating and emergent.

If you hold some soil from the garden in your hand, although not obvious you would be holding one of the foundations of life itself. This small amount of soil will be teeming with millions of bacteria and microorganisms that are part of a complex system responsible for sustaining life on our planet. The most important insight is the acknowledgement that networks are the fundamental pattern of organization of all living systems. The important point is that there are no elaborate rules by which the system works. Moreover, there is no one in charge. The system works because of a few simple principles.

Of Welsh Farmers and Complex Systems

In September 2000, inspired by French protests over fuel prices, a small group of Welsh farmers hatched a plan in a small cattle market in North Wales. The ringleader was Brynle Williams, a local livestock farmer from Cilcain. The plan was to start blockading the roads outside the Stanlow refinery, near Ellesmere Port.

Now a few Welsh farmers may not have the power to influence a refinery or the fuel prices in the country, but an interesting series of events followed once they launched their (relatively small) plan. Passing truck drivers who could see the farmers protesting against fuel prices started honking in solidarity, and that encouraged the farmers' protest to grow. As the Stanlow protest grew, the farmers got bolder and prevented many tankers from leaving the refinery.

That, in turn, encouraged the truck drivers and the hauliers to join in the protest and they threatened to block the major motorway junctions in the UK. Other farmers and hauliers from North West England soon joined the Stanlow strikes.

The next day, farmers and hauliers began demonstrating at the Pembroke oil refinery, the Hemel Hempstead oil terminal and in Gateshead. And a slow convoy of 100 lorries and tractors caused tailbacks on the A1, replicating what had happened in France. By the end of the week, all the major oil refineries and depots in Wales and North West England had been blockaded. By Monday, 11 September 2000, demonstrations at oil depots had spread to Scotland and southern England. With the threat of gas stations running dry, motorists did a run on the petrol stations and, indeed, they started running dry. Many shops began to run out of bread, milk and fresh food, and the NHS was put on red alert as supplies began running low and operations were cancelled.

All this because a ragtag outfit of a few Welsh farmers demonstrated outside the Stanlow refinery in North Wales.

What Makes a System Complex?

This story provides an evocative example of a complex system in operation. We can try to understand it by examining three attributes of complex systems – attributes that are key to understanding complexity theory:

1. SELF-ORGANIZING: The system consists of a number of diverse agents and each of those agents makes decisions on how to behave. The farmers and the truckers were diverse agents. Neither did the farmers intend to bring the UK fuel supplies to a standstill,

nor did they have the power or the resources to do so. What happened with the truckers joining in was a case of spontaneous self-organization

2. ADAPTIVE: The diverse agents interact with each other thereby making the system 'adaptive'. The system of the farmers and truckers became an adaptive system. The outcome was not planned, but the adaptive system was now dynamically responding to changes in the environment and opening up new possibilities

3. EMERGENT: The system emerges as it takes on wholly different qualities and produces unexpected outcomes resulting from the pattern of interactions which no one organization or individual can control. What happened as a result of the initial actions was completely unpredictable and therefore 'emergent', for example the run on the filling stations by motorists

We chose to use this story as an example of how complex systems work. Although social media had not yet arrived, the farmers and the truckers kept in touch using their mobile phones, and the ability to communicate speedily was a significant factor in the formation of the complex system that developed. Think of what 21st century digital technology can do.

Developing a Systems Perspective

In the interdependent and interconnected 21st century we need to make some significant shifts in the way we think and the way we lead in complex systems. We have to make a significant leap from our old, linear ways of thinking to developing what is called a 'systems' perspective. This means:

1. We are able to recognize and accept that we work in systems that are complex and dynamic, and they are made up of interdependencies and interconnections that are not in our control

2. We are able to understand that the whole is much more than the sum of its parts; that is why, without understanding how others think and see things, our solutions will always be limited

3. We are able to step back and perceive both short-term and long-term perspectives and find ways of balancing them

4. We are able to take into account both measurable and non-measurable factors in addressing the complexity we face. So, while data is useful, so is pattern recognition, judgment and intuitive thinking

5. We are able to see our role in the system and find ways of influencing the system to change; we are not victims of the system, rather we have what psychologists call 'agency' to make change happen

You are probably thinking there is nothing new in this and that many leaders have been doing this for ages. That is somewhat true. However, while in earlier times we had the luxury of ignoring a systems perspective, we could still be reasonably successful as a business. This is becoming increasingly difficult. The reason is that the world in which we live and work has become significantly more complex than it used to be in the previous century, not least because it is exponentially more interconnected. This is making systemic perspectives a key leadership ability. Take a look at some of the critical changes that are taking place in front of our eyes:

a) Information itself is fast becoming a commodity and it no longer presents a significant advantage. Instead, the ability for insight through collaboratively working across boundaries is becoming a source of advantage

b) Digital technology is enabling large ecosystems to thrive, which means that understanding the patterns that connect the ecosystem together is becoming critical

c) Anyone with access to information and a digital device can express a point of view and share it globally and instantaneously (we call this socially created information). As the authors of *The Social Leader*[40] wrote, "There is simply no place to hide."

d) The issues we face as leaders are becoming increasingly more complex and global, requiring a very different mindset

e) A new millennial generation is demanding higher transparency, higher engagement and a culture that values diversity, openness and entrepreneurship

What does all this mean for us who are trying to shift our organizations into the 21st century? Well, for one, we have to become agile and adaptive in the way we think about our challenges and respond to them. This means working with a mindset that is able to draw upon multiple perspectives, diversity and cross-functional approaches.

Second, we have to become much more integrative in our approach; for example, in our roles we may belong to one function, but we have to understand our role and work from a systems perspective in which every other function is interconnected and interdependent. We must also shift our emphasis from the old industrial age practice of achieving efficiency through top-down control to learning to work collaboratively without knowing all the answers.

In other words, we have to learn to appreciate a phenomenon called emergence in which the answers emerge through a process of engagement and dialogue with diverse groups of people whose opinions may differ from ours!

Similarly, from an external perspective, we must integrate profits and sustainability. Sustainability is not CSR but an integral element of the way we work. All this points to one important message: we have to learn to think and respond systemically in a complex world. What exactly does it mean for us to become systemic thinkers?

Learning to Step Back

Systemic thinking is, first and foremost, about becoming aware of the 'whole picture'. Imagine the difference between being one of the dancers on the dance floor and then stepping back to a place from where you see the dance. Both are important, but what happens in our workplaces is that we get so lost in the detail and of feeling like being a small part. We consistently forget to step back and see the dance![41]

It is only when we step back that we begin to see the interrelationships and interdependencies that form the whole system. The functions, the roles, customers, the competition, the alliances and all the stakeholders, they are all part of the larger system in which we must thrive! Now imagine that every employee in your organization is able to see how his or her role is such an important part of this system and how that begins to shift their perspective! People change their behaviours when they are able to see the bigger picture of their setting!

A systems perspective is also, therefore, being able to perceive the world through the eyes of the other person. This is empathy, the ability to put yourself in the other person's shoes – be that a customer, a colleague, someone in a cross-functional team – and address the issue from this valuable other-perspective!

That is why a systems perspective doesn't just jump into solving problems, but allows us to step back and look at the larger system. This means incorporating other points of view, however diverse and divergent they are! It doesn't mean that we listen to everybody and end up not taking decisions; rather, it means that we are quickly able to make sense of the complexity of the problem by stepping back and then getting the right people into the room and addressing the problem. This is why collaboration becomes a very important part of this perspective.

Now comes the most important part of the systems perspective: all of us have the ability to influence large systems! We can do this by making subtle and intelligent shifts in our conversations, actions and behaviours so that they are amplified as they spread. For example, when Nelson Mandela put on the colours of the Springboks Rugby team and walked into the centre of Cape Town stadium, his action generated a spontaneous outflow of positive emotion that went a long way towards healing the painful history of apartheid. Similarly, a meaningful conversation has the ability to generate effects beyond the scope of the conversation. Powerful leadership behaviours invite others into their wake, thus creating new leverage points for change.

Overcoming Systems Blindness

The question is, can we learn to develop a systems perspective? The answer is yes. But first we have to become aware of our systems blindness. You can see that in the way we jump to a conclusion or all agree to a specific action at a meeting, without stepping back to understand the interdependencies and interconnections. So we end up being blind to what is called the unintended consequence. So pervasive is this habit that we don't even notice it. And just because most of the others are doing the same thing, it gives us the illusion of reality. So the first thing to practise is the art of stepping back and taking some time to explore the bigger picture, while being aware of your instant reactions. The next time you are in a meeting, try this out.

The second thing to do is to develop a new habit of inquiry: the art of asking meaningful questions that prevent the familiar slide into reactive thinking. Meaningful questions also create the pause and the space for others around you to start becoming aware of the bigger system. So, a question such as, 'what is the outcome we need to create?' is a question that helps us move away from our internal biases of thinking to the output that is needed. All too often, our problem-solving stops at precisely that – an examination of the superficial level of events, or the stuff that happens around us. So if we perceive a drop in sales as an event, we are then more than likely to react to that event by a stop-gap solution. But that solution has consequences in the medium term and also has an impact on the other functions in the organization.

Moreover, if the other functions are also using stop-gap solutions, there is an amplifiable negative loop being created that will require further stop-gap solutions! We have to shift from focusing on the event – which only allows us to react – to paying attention to the deeper structures driving those events. We can then begin to perceive patterns through questions such as, 'why does this happen?', and 'what is it about the way we think and plan that allows this to happen?' A conversation around such questions leads us to understand the deeper issues at play and then find ways of making changes. We discover ways not just to solve problems, but to *create*.[42]

As you can see, there are some big hurdles we must overcome: first, a tendency for a reactive mindset that is driven by wanting short-term solutions. Moreover, under the pressure of time we tend to lapse into what we know and what we have tried before, which is therefore biased. The second hurdle is of going at it alone and ignoring the interconnections and interdependencies in the larger system. It is certainly more efficient to do it this way, but hardly effective. The third hurdle is of not knowing the answer or the way to get there and being unable to manage the ambiguity. Our brains are not great at dealing with ambiguity and we would rather do something quick than allow the solution to emerge from conversations with other functions. The fourth and final hurdle is about power: to work effectively in a system, we have to let go of our old, industrial age perceptions of power. Power from a systemic perspective is defined by how we contribute to the overall benefit of the system.

A systems perspective is about doing all these things: it is about making significant shifts in our conversations, actions and behaviours. Most importantly, it is about developing a mindset that is able to be mindful rather than reactive. And it all begins by learning to step back!

The 21st Century as a Complex System

A digitally wired 21st century is a complex system. We are going to need an entirely different mindset to navigate this system and the old rules of running our organizations are not going to work. Digital disruptions, unprecedented business models and operating in a landscape where the old rules no longer work is forcing us to throw out the old playbook of management. Instead we are being challenged to embrace a new world of adaptability. The leadership demands on the 21st century leader are substantially different from those experienced by the 20th century leader:

1. The 21st century leader will have to learn to operate in far more ambiguity than ever before. As we said before, this is a strange paradox given that we have more information available than ever. While rules and procedures provided the light in the 20th century organization, we will now need new guardrails for dealing with ambiguity. Our research indicates that a higher purpose, both at the individual and the organizational level, provides these guardrails. This is because purpose provides a stable anchor to help people step back, take a wider view and ask broader questions, the most fundamental of which is 'why?'.

2. The 21st century leader will have to learn to use attention very differently from what we have been used to in the past. How we perceive, interpret and respond will become the new determinants of our success. The fact is that we do not use our attention resources well. This is further compounded by the supercomputers we carry around that are diminishing our attention capacities faster than ever before. Leaders will have to embrace greater mindfulness and curiosity to cope with this newfound attention deficit in the midst of ambiguity. By framing our organizations in the context of the broader system in which it thrives, purpose creates the space for higher levels of attention because it embraces holism and thus helps us identify what really matters.

3. The 21st century leader will have to operate in increasingly complex environments with empathy. Purpose is the key vehicle for leaders as they are called to create

meaning in organizational life. Also, because purpose is fundamentally about service, it naturally encourages leaders to embrace a more empathetic mindset.

Developing a systems perspective is one antidote to the blindness that keeps us from rehumanizing our organizations.

Terminally ill and with less than two years before she finally succumbed to her cancer in June 1962, Rachel Carson did a commencement address at Scripps College in California. She told the graduates, "Today our whole Earth has become only another shore from which we look out across the dark ocean of space, uncertain what we shall find when we sail out among the stars … your generation must come to terms with the environment. You must face realities instead of taking refuge in ignorance and evasion of truth. Yours is a grave and sobering responsibility, but it is also a shining opportunity. You go out into a world where mankind is challenged, as it has never been challenged before, to prove its maturity and its mastery – not of nature, but of itself. Therein lies our hope and our destiny."[43]

It is important to look at some of the other traps and pitfalls that leaders in 21ˢᵗ century organizations must navigate. We now turn our attention to those.

CHAPTER 5

Navigating Organizational Traps in the 21st Century

"The courageous conversation is the one you don't want to have."
DAVID WHYTE

We are sitting in an off-site crisis meeting of senior executives from a leading FMCG company. The CEO is talking about a burning platform comprised of a drop in sales, customers switching loyalties, the lack of innovation inside the company and the threat of disruption to their business models by smaller, agile players. The big reason why they are assembled in the 'war room', as the CEO calls it, is because the analysts have published a highly critical report with a very pessimistic outlook about the future. "Their heydays are clearly over", was how the report began and it proceeded to criticize the strategy and the culture at this company. "We have been rewarding the culture of silos and that's why we lack in collaboration," said the Head of HR. "The real problem is that we don't have a clear digital strategy and our competition is way ahead of us," said the CEO. Then, looking at the Head of Marketing, he continued, "We are wasting millions in television adverts. We need a digital transformation." The Head of Sales and the Head of Supply Chain are engaged in a side conversation and we can see the Head of Sales shaking her head. The CEO turns to her and asks with some irritation, "Can we have one conversation please? Tina, what's up?" "It's the same old issues," replied Tina. "We need some bold actions. We need to rally the troops behind us."

This conversation could be taking place in any organization, anywhere in the world. By the end of the day, the executive team had reworked their strategy and had come up with a list of actions. When they met for dinner that evening their mood was upbeat. In the following few days, we interviewed several people further down in the organization who expressed their cynicism about the ability of their company to change.

The real problem in this company was not a lack of strategy, or even a list of actions. The problem was the three traps that the executives kept falling into.

Trap 1: The Control Trap

We built the 20th century organization for stability and efficiency, not for being responsive in a fast-moving 21st century. The better the control, the higher the efficiency. In a relatively slower and less interconnected world that operated around sovereign nation states and local economies, the 20th century organization thrived. The assets that were owned by the organizations came to define their strength and resilience. Assets were not just land, labour and capital, they represented a mindset of feudal ownership. And assets had to be protected and controlled, which is why so much of our organizational structure, even today, is built around a fortification perspective: protect against change, build strong walls, delineate the departments and functions, guard your intellectual property, recruit and retain the best people, manage performance and a whole plethora of terms and concepts that we created. Management was largely speaking the science of maintaining control and order, as that was what was best for stability. That meant building rigid hierarchies and the processes that go with them: top-down communication lines, management by division of work, strong internal boundaries between departments and functions, centralized control systems, etc. This model worked for quite a long time because the context was relatively stable and power could be centralized in the hands of a few.

It doesn't take much imagination to figure out why so many of our organizations are struggling in the 21st century. The context has changed dramatically over the past 15 years and continues to do so. Digital technology, global information flows, a new mindset of transparency and immediacy and a generation unencumbered by the 20th century mindset are taking apart the familiar world of the 20th century. Nowhere before in human history have we experienced the scale and pace that we are doing now. Moreover, we are globally wired up in a way that was hitherto unimaginable. But what makes the 21st century significantly different from the past is that this is the first time in human history that the technology that is changing the world is being developed and controlled, not by big institutions of government and industry, but by the new generations. The gap between the world that digital technology is wiring up and the world that many of us are holding on to from a 20th century perspective is reaching unsustainable proportions.

Focus on Efficiency

Ask any CEO what they want their organization to be and you hear the same words everywhere: agile, adaptable, nimble, responsive, innovative, being able to navigate complexity, etc.

Every top management team thinks that there are too many dysfunctional processes inside their organization that are coming in the way of speedy decision-making. Everyone complains about how slow their organizations are and the tired oil tanker versus speedboat metaphor gets thrown in for effect. Consultancies offer solutions for simplification, agility, innovation culture and everything else under the sun. Yet the elephant in the room stays unchallenged: the 20th century organization was simply not built for agility, adaptability and all the wonderful words we've used above. The 20th century management habits we learned were not geared for transparency and innovation. Let's face it: so many of the leadership models that we learned to practise are simply out of touch with 21st century reality. It is time to call out the elephant in the room.

Most of our 20th century organizations were built around the premise of efficiency. The problem is not with efficiency per se, but the factors that develop once we build the structures for efficiency. In purely engineering terms, efficiency is maximized when the numerator of output is significantly greater than the denominator of input. When you translate that into human terms, any process becomes efficient when the input denominator is controlled by maximizing uniformity and compliance and by minimizing risk and variation. As long as we can ensure that these factors are kept to a minimum, we raise efficiency. What works beautifully on a machine, however, translates badly into human terms. So minimizing diversity and maximizing compliance is a great strategy for increasing efficiency. Notwithstanding the human element, we can continue to be efficient if that is the ultimate goal and disregard the human cost, as long as the overall system is compatible with our drive for efficiency. Take that away and the efficiency mindset breaks down instantly. What works with ease and excellence when all you want to do is increase the output to input ratio utterly fails when you want some creativity, collaboration or innovation from your people. In this instance, the goal is the opposite: *maximize* variation and *minimize* uniformity. When the world stayed somewhat stable for relatively longer periods of time and when all you had to do was deliver solutions to known problems, the efficiency mindset worked fine. No longer.

Carrot and Stick

Even performance motivators become an issue, as Daniel Pink illustrated so evocatively in his early book, *Drive*.[44] "If you want someone to do manual work faster, pay that person more and you get it done," Pink said. But if the work is knowledge work, paying people more will only cost you more as the carrot reward system fails to work. What people are motivated by – once you have paid them enough – are factors that have nothing to do with money, but are more about purpose, belonging and a sense of meaning.

A related problem to the efficiency trap is the need to control. We ran an innovation workshop recently for a large software company in India that was handling the back-office work for a well-known US pharmaceutical company. The Chief Technology Officer (CTO), who was new to the role, said in his opening remark, "Since taking charge three months ago, I have been picking up lots of issues that need to be addressed." The term 'taking charge' is such a hangover, not just from the 20th century but from an industrial age mindset that was, in turn, borne out of the military model. The CTO was blind to his own vocabulary and to the deeper unconscious biases that resided in his cognitive processes and he needed to be reminded of the same.

Control and Conformity

The problem is that so many of our internal structures are set up precisely for control. The hierarchy is the most visible one but the list includes so much more, like the way communication channels operate, the way performance is managed, the way we run our meetings, the way we structure the office space, etc. Once again, control is fine as long as the environment you are operating in is amenable to control. In complex environments, we have to learn to 'control' differently. As the philosopher Alan Watts put it, "… when you swim, you don't grab hold of the water, because if you do you will sink."[45] What we can grab hold of and control are the mechanics of running an organization, and there is a need for control when it comes to so much. But that is the routine stuff. If you want people to think of new solutions to new 21st century problems, don't smother them with rules. Raise the bar much higher and give them the handrails of purpose, show them how empathy operates and create the space for them to find meaning in their work and their relationships. That's when the organization starts swimming!

A related problem is conformity. The need to conform is a primeval human need lodged deep inside our evolutionary brain. Conformity to a group brings certain advantages such as fostering a sense of belonging. However, beyond the social glue that conformity provides, it becomes a dangerous slippery slope. 'Are we all on the same page?' is a great question to ask if we are asking our people if they are committed to a goal when there is an emergency and when we want people to do exactly what the playbook says. It becomes a dumb question when we are operating in a complex environment and we want our people to think independently. Remember the scene from the old classic, *Apollo 13*? The genius of Gene Kranz, the mission director, was not so much in the way he motivated his team to work on the problem, but in the way he was able to tear up the are-we-on-the-same-page need and invite a dissenting voice from a junior team member. The common purpose was to bring back the stricken spacecraft, but the solution came from productive dissent.

Trap 2: The Power Trap

Pushed to meet their targets, more than 5,000 employees at Wells Fargo created over two million fake bank and credit card accounts which were used to charge fees. According to a September 2016 report from the Consumer Financial Protection Bureau (CFPB), "Today we fined Wells Fargo Bank $100 million for widespread unlawful sales practices. The bank's employees secretly opened accounts and shifted funds from consumers' existing accounts into these new accounts without their knowledge or permission to do so, often racking up fees or other charges."[46] At a Congressional Hearing on 29 September 2016, CEO John Stumpf was forced to apologize, but reports about the event that took place confirm that Stumpf appeared remorseless and clueless about what was going on.

Power Blinds

Dominique Strauss-Kahn, or DSK as he was known, the Head of the International Monetary Fund was the leading contender to run against Nicolas Sarkozy in the 2012 French Presidential campaign. On 14 May 2011, he was arrested on charges of a criminal sexual act, attempted rape and an unlawful imprisonment in connection with a sexual assault, according to the New York Police Department. The police escorted him off an Air France flight headed to

Paris for questioning about the alleged sexual assault of a Sofitel Hotel housekeeping employee. He was later indicted on seven counts: two counts of a criminal sexual act, two counts of sexual abuse and one count each of attempt to commit rape, unlawful imprisonment and forcible touching. Strauss-Kahn was a powerful man, used to mixing with presidents and prime ministers. He was a brilliant economist and was seen as the leading presidential candidate. The question is what makes someone like Strauss-Kahn assault a hotel worker in the Presidential Suite of the Sofitel hotel?

On 9 December 2009, the tabloid *New York Post* published the salacious text messages between Tiger Woods and Jaimee Grubbs, a Californian waitress. Another set of text messages between Tiger Woods and Joslyn James, a porn star, was published on 8 March 2010. The messages were clearly from Woods's phone and, in both instances, the transcripts had been sold to tabloids. Why did Tiger Woods – who had such an enormous international reputation to protect – not see the risk of sending text messages from his phone?

The Perils of Power

What is the link between Stumpf, DSK and Tiger Woods? All three were victims of 'powerfulness'. Not power, but powerfulness. Power is important to get things done and using power wisely and appropriately has always been the hallmark of character in leaders. But feeling powerful is a totally different thing. The problem with the 20th century organizations is that we built them upon existing, old feudal structures and made 'feeling powerful' a perk and a benefit. Dedicated parking spaces, executive bathrooms, executive dining rooms, to name just a few, were not just symbols of power, they were meant to be symbols of powerfulness.

The 'do you know who I am?' question became the throwaway line meant to convey powerfulness. Quite apart from the fact that people who behave this way have always been perceived as obnoxious, there is increasingly little room for them in the flatter, knowledge-intensive organizations of the 21st century. For one, the new generations generally do not subscribe to this view of conferred power and, even more importantly, the market does not either. Even more problematic, however, is the fact that powerfulness diminishes empathetic activity in the human brain.

Power and Empathy

Dacher Keltner, a psychology professor at University of California, Berkeley, has been studying power for over two decades, more specifically how subjects under the influence of power were prone to becoming impulsive and unaware of risk. Keltner's research demonstrates how the influence of power substantially diminishes the human ability to empathize.[47] Power corrupts and absolute power corrupts absolutely, as the old adage goes, and is clearly borne out by recent neurological research.

Sukhvinder Obhi is a cognitive neuroscientist at McMaster University in Canada and has been studying the effect of power on human beings. According to Obhi, power has a profound effect on the neurocognitive system underlying behaviour. "We have identified effects of power on the tendency to mirror observed actions, the way in which emotions are recognized in facial expressions and bodily postures, the manner in which same and opposite sex individuals are perceived and the tendency to feel in control over outcomes."[48] Mirroring each other is a vital behaviour that human beings engage in to demonstrate empathy, also known as perspective taking.

Obhi's research is ground-breaking in that he and his colleagues were able to demonstrate that power changes how the brain responds to others.

Power and Emotions

Michael Kraus, a psychologist at Yale University, found that those who were higher in social class (as determined by level of education) among full-time employees of a public university, were less able to accurately identify emotions in photographs of human faces than were co-workers who were lower in social class.[49] Clearly, social power has an impact on reading into the emotions of other people. There could be a simple explanation for this: Princeton psychologist Susan Fiske feels that powerful people are not skilled at attending to others around them because they do not need them.[50] Whatever the explanation may be, much of the research in this field indicates that power has an impact on our ability to empathize with others.

We built many of our 20th century structures and edifices on the foundations of conferred top-down power. The many vertical work layers, the staircase to promotions with the job titles with status apparently increasing with every rung, the corner offices, the entitlements, the list continues. Conferred power became a means to reward people inside organizations and job titles provided identity. In fact, the classic 20th century organizational pyramid was but a reflection of feudal structures with the very few people at the top controlling the rest of the organization. As a result, knowledge had to be tightly protected and given out on a need-to-know basis.

The gap between knowing and doing that so many companies experience owes itself to the pyramidal hierarchy. In the 20th century organization, knowing was the job of the top and doing was the job of the rest of the organization.

What confuses people is that they are not being asked to take initiative and be proactive, but the reward and performance structures around them continue to be top-down. *Unboss*, the title of a book by Kolind and Bøtter[51] is a great idea about a new mindset that overturns conventional understanding of management and work on its head. It fits neatly into the 21st century worldview. But it needs a lot of work on the culture of the organization to help people change a mindset. And, of course, we need to work on the structures of power.

Trap 3: The Attention Trap

Tim Munden, Chief Learning Officer at Unilever, is on a crusade about attention and mindfulness. As someone who has been entrusted with developing Unilever's leaders, he sees inattention as the biggest problem we need to fix as we move into ever more distractions in the hyper-connected 21st century. We recently watched him run a mindfulness session at the start of a Unilever strategy session that included all the members of the Unilever executive team. It was quite a sight to watch 120 people sit still in meditation. Quoting Viktor E. Frankl, he talks animatedly about the space between stimulus and our reaction to the stimulus that we have to learn to manage. He now runs regular retreats at Four Acres, the Unilever learning facility to help managers develop focus and attention. The retreats are sold out and there is a waiting list. The one thing you have to do when you walk into the retreat? Give up your phones. As Simone Weil said, "Attention is the rarest and purest form of generosity."[52]

The fact is most human beings are not great at paying attention. Attention is like a muscle and needs to be trained.

Many of us pick up habits of inattention that also, unfortunately, get reinforced in workplaces and organizations as we watch senior leaders do the same and get rewarded for them. Attention is literally what we attend to, and what we attend to is what becomes reality.

Cognitive Depletion

Attention is what connects us to the world, and it shapes and moulds our experience of the world. The problem of attention is compounded by the fact that we are being inundated non-stop by information in a way that we have never known before. To repeat, more information was created in this century than the sum total of all information created until then. Our digital devices are an open gateway to the world and the deluge comes our way incessantly. As the deluge starts competing to get our attention, it forces us into instant gratification. This means our brains are now hooked to short-term rewards for flicking from one thing to the other. And before we know it, we have drowned in inattention.

One more thing: attention is not unlimited and we can run out of it, producing attention-deficit and what psychologists refer to as cognitive depletion. How we conserve attention depends on how we use it. Practices like 'multi-tasking' that brainwashed an entire generation add to the sorry state of affairs. Repeated switching between one thing and the other, which is what digital devices tend to get us to do, is the hungriest of attention-consuming behaviours. In fact, anything that gets us to multi-task or indulge in continual switching – like being on conference calls and answering emails at the same time – increases stress and saps attention. Cognitive depletion is a growing phenomenon and it is alarming how so many leaders that we have interviewed in the past couple of years have fallen into this trap.

Mindlessness

The more serious problem with attention-deficit or cognitive depletion is what it does to you. Alison is a senior administrator in the National Health Service in the UK. She was telling us about how tired she routinely gets in the afternoons and she can feel her brain hurting. When we asked her to describe her day, it was a relentless march of one thing after another with no breaks in between. Three or four back-to-back meetings, constant checks on the phone for emails, text messages and WhatsApp messages, checking project reports, phone calls, team members dropping into the office with a question or two, lots of coffee, team meetings and *the usual politics*. And all this before it is even lunchtime! A routine like this forces your brain into operating from biases and shortcuts as that is nature's way of getting you to conserve energy. This shortcut has its advantage in that you are able to function despite being depleted cognitively; the problem is that your responses are going to be reactive, knee-jerk and not thought through. In other words, you are operating mindlessly.

Becoming Selfish

But that is not the whole story. Working for long periods of time in a state of cognitive depletion also makes you 'selfish',[53] a term used by Daniel Kahneman, winner of the Nobel Prize in Economic Sciences in 2002. What Kahneman meant by selfish was the inability to empathize, listen or be open to other perspectives. Alison immediately jumped on this information that we gave her and spoke about the feedback she had been receiving for a while. "It's exactly as you are saying," Alison remarked. "My team tells me I don't listen to them."

A Tale of Two Centuries

The three traps – control, power and attention – keep us squarely imprisoned in the 20ᵗʰ century organization. Lacking awareness, we are likely to walk into them. We call them traps for that simple reason. 21ˢᵗ century organizations are built on a very different logic. Fewer hierarchies, a more equitable distribution of power and a deep and powerful sense of purpose.

But all this is fine if you have a 21ˢᵗ century organization is probably what many of you are thinking. What happens to the 20ᵗʰ century organization that was built around hierarchies and top-down communication? The question is not whether you are in a 20ᵗʰ century organization or a 21ˢᵗ century one. The real challenge is about creating 21ˢᵗ century initiatives inside the 20ᵗʰ century organization, experimenting with new ideas and expanding the limits of what is possible. We will explore this in more detail in the next few chapters.

CHAPTER 6

The 21st Century Business Opportunity for Purpose

"Make your work to be in keeping with your purpose."

LEONARDO DA VINCI

Doing the Right Thing

With the ending of apartheid in 1994, Nelson Mandela became the first president of an independent republic. His party, the African National Congress (ANC), was in power and the very first act they wanted to pass was to abolish rugby. For the black people of South Africa, rugby was not just a game, but a deeply hated symbol of apartheid. Black people did not play rugby and did not watch rugby; the green and gold colours that the South African national rugby union team – the Springboks – wore were the colours of hatred and centuries of division. So what better way to retaliate against all the horrors of apartheid than to ban the game once and for all? Revenge, after all, is the basic emotion underscoring human conflict, the dominant *leitmotif* in a primitive human algorithm that is hardwired into the human mind. Only one person stood in the way.

A free South Africa went on to host the Rugby World Cup in 1995 and, against all odds, the national team made their way into the finals. On a clear winter's day in the Ellis Park stadium in Johannesburg, the two teams had run onto the field. The Springboks were playing against the favourites to win, the New Zealand All Blacks. Then, suddenly, Mandela was seen walking to the centre of the stadium wearing a Springboks cap and a jersey with the number six on the back, the same as worn by the captain of the Springboks, Francois Pienaar. As Mandela shook the hands of the players, the chants of "Nelson, Nelson, Nelson ..." began to resonate loudly through the stadium. A year into democracy, a new country was born on a rugby field. The words of the Archbishop Desmond Tutu said it all: "I believe that that was a defining moment in the life of our country. He has a knack of doing just the right thing and being able to carry it off with aplomb."

What complex evolutionary algorithm in the human brain goes into the decision to do the right thing? We may never know the answer to this question. What we do know is that in order to do the right thing we have to consciously overcome deep-seated default biases and habits that stand in the way. The 'need to be right' is one such bias; overbearing and powerful, it can easily sabotage the action of doing the right thing.

Doing the right thing is essentially a human quality, but not human in a hard-wired, unconscious way; rather it is borne out of the mindful mindset and a sharp and unwavering awareness of what is required to be done. Mandela's greatest achievement as a leader was not in helping to liberate South Africa from apartheid; that was the result of so many small cumulative actions that all played their role, including the actions of his predecessor, F.W. de Klerk. His greatest triumph came in his years in Robben Island prison, his home for 27 years. From his original intention of freeing

South Africa from the white Afrikaners, he made the journey to the other side of the valley, the place of purpose. In that place, the vision of the Rainbow Nation was born: 'freedom from' had transcended into 'freedom for'.

Moving from 'needing to be right' 'doing the right thing' takes a wider view of the world and one's place in it. That is why this is the greatest leadership journey of all. It requires expansive thinking and moving to a higher place, despite what your immediate needs and wants dictate to you. Three things stand out in this most human of all trajectories:

1. *Crafting and retaining a clear sense of purpose that emerges out of what is needed rather than what one wants*
2. *Empathizing at deep levels and being able to understand a situation from multiple perspectives*
3. *Designing solutions from a place that generates meaning for others*

To Lead is to Care

For us, the act of rehumanizing leadership begins with a word that is hardly ever used at the workplace: to care. To care is to deeply understand the purpose behind why we do what we do, and to bring that sense of purpose into every leadership conversation we have, every leadership action we take and every leadership behaviour we display. To care is also to help create meaning for others we engage with, be they our colleagues and team workers, suppliers, clients and customers, or the people in our communities and societies. To care is to give attention and energy to what we do as leaders. As Paul Polman, former CEO of Unilever, says when it comes to addressing the dilemma of making profits while living the purpose of sustainability, "If you really cared, you would know what to do. You have to care for the environment, for your people, for your consumers and for your business."

For too long the myth has endured that business is about anything but caring. It has now been four decades since Milton Friedman won the Nobel Prize in economics and shaped the dominant narrative that the role of a business is to make more money for its shareholders. As we stated earlier, Friedman wrote that the sole social responsibility of a business is to maximize its profits. For a company to pursue anything other than profit would be tantamount to "pure and unadulterated socialism", he wrote in his 1970 essay. Friedman's theory ended up legitimizing greed by giving it the rationale of market economics.

As we wrote earlier, this myth is reaching the end of its usefulness. Profits are important and necessary, but only as a means of sustaining something far more important and useful. Rehumanizing leadership in the 21st century is the practice of an alternative narrative: that profits and purpose go hand in hand. Anything short of this narrative is doomed to failure. Purpose is no longer something that is good to have: it might well become the key differentiator between success and failure.

It has been over ten years since the financial crisis. Movements such as Occupy Wall Street were attempts to chip away at the profit-at-all-costs approach of unbridled capitalism. Today, a new worldview is dawning, despite President Trump's populist attempts at cutting corporate tax and promoting profits.

Resurrecting Purpose

Financial Times journalist Andrew Edgecliffe-Johnson (4 January 2019) writes about the big changes taking place and takes the example of BlackRock's investor Larry Fink who has $6.3 tn of assets. According to Edgecliffe-Johnson, Fink wrote that with governments failing to prepare for the future, people were looking to companies to deliver not only financial performance but a positive contribution to society, benefiting customers and communities as well as shareholders. He goes on to quote Fink further and writes that without a social purpose companies fail to make the investments in employees, innovation and capital expenditures needed for long-term growth and above-par returns to the likes of BlackRock.

The old system is starting to show the first cracks. The legacy of industrial age practices in the way we manage our organizations is reaching the end of its usefulness. When we met with Shayne Elliott, the CEO of Australia New Zealand Banking Group Ltd, and asked him about the role of purpose at ANZ and the journey to get there, this is what he had to say: "The system hasn't really delivered. Big business gave us the Global Financial Crisis (GFC) and the fat cats. The system was supposed to 'trickle down' but it hasn't been that way for most people. We at ANZ have to reconnect with society and community, otherwise we're in peril ... I am as well." When asked if purpose and business dividend can go together, Elliott added, "We will be a more attractive option for employees and customers. And, with an authentic purpose, maybe customers will forgive us more readily when we make mistakes. It might even affect the degree of scrutiny we get from regulators."

What Elliott is talking about is trust and the absence of it, especially in the banking sector. But this is not someone trying to pay lip-service to purpose; behind this statement lies a genuine care for not just the customers of the bank, but for society at large.

Elliott spoke about why the strong anti-business movement in Australia is legitimate and why the system feels broken for so many ordinary people. "If I work really hard and send my kids to the best schools, I and my kids have a shot at a better life and to really make it. Even if I sweep the floor, I have a chance that my kids will work on Wall Street. With this in the background, people didn't care if companies made a lot of money as long as they could participate. What happened was that it didn't work out, at least that's the perception. Now it's 'my kids can't get a job'. It feels rigged."

The need to relate to the community and society are strategically important for any business, as it must fundamentally care for the people it serves. Too often, Elliott feels that as institutions grow and become successful they forget what they were originally all about.

Our work with Elliott and his team has been a shared journey of taking his organization to articulating that very purpose. From a 'little idea', as Elliott calls it, the story of ANZ's purpose and its integration with business has become a successful story.

Rehumanizing Banking

Elliott refers to the dehumanizing way in which banks talk to the public using numbers and profit share. Referring to the 'boys club' effect, he talks of how some companies throw money at charities as a reaction, but that doesn't work because it's not authentic and people can tell that 'you're just trying to appease us'.

As a banker, he is being unconventional in his criticism of our attachment to metrics and the dehumanization that the language itself brings with it. "Banks want to live by metrics", Elliott says animatedly, "Look, judgment is hard to do. Metrics allow us to avoid judgment. But this is an incomplete way to manage yourself." It is interesting when you look at the news. Everything seems to be measured in economic value, for example: 'The economic cost of domestic violence is ...' or 'The economic cost of migration is ...' This is utterly dehumanizing, according to Elliott. He carries on: "To make matters worse, we in big businesses talk to the public in very unappealing ways: numbers, profits, shares. These are things they don't care about."

Elliott refers to how he is not the solitary warrior waging war on metrics. He speaks of Neville Power, the CEO of Fortescue, and their conversations on the Business Council of Australia having lost its way. "It has become a cold, metrics-driven lobby group. Why are big businesses lobbying for lower corporate taxes? In the face of all the issues we've talked about, this looks just awful. We refused to put money into that campaign."

We needed to probe deeper as this was turning out to be an important conversation. Our next question was whether Elliott's decision to not put money into a campaign for lower corporate taxes was influenced by the purpose journey that ANZ was on. "Of course," came the reply. "Purpose was in the back of our mind when we made that decision. We felt that the decision needed to be about fairness. We feel that we're able to pay our taxes as long as the system is fair. Interestingly, the head of the Australian Tax Office did a study to find out about tax evasion. They discovered that the biggest problem they have is transparency.

The study found that people generally pay their taxes until they find out that someone else isn't. Then it becomes about fairness: 'They're not paying taxes, why should I?'"

Back to Doing the Right Thing

Elliott tells the story of one of ANZ's customers, who is now one of the richest men in Australia with a personal net worth of $1.2 bn. His name is Solomon Lew and he is fond of saying, "I'll never change my religion, I'll never change my football club and I'll never change my bank." Elliott tells this story with great relish and takes us right back to the time when Lew's father had died when Lew was young and Lew wanted to start a business. "He went to ANZ and wanted to borrow £5,000 against his mother's house." The ANZ bank manager refused to let him mortgage his house and instead told him, "I'll give you £2,000 unsecured." Elliott leans back in his chair and says, "That is why today we have an over 50-year relationship with one of the wealthiest men in Australia. But that is not why we did it. We did it because it was the right thing to do."

Our conversation with Elliott turned to leadership and we asked him how the journey of purpose at ANZ he has been on has shaped his own views. Elliott was quick to point out that this was not new to him as a leader, "but it has strengthened my idea that there needed to be something more than just shareholder returns guiding us. I think longer term and I think it has made me really think about the decisions." We went on to ask him if shareholders will notice or even give him credit for his purpose effort. Elliott was quick to retort: "I think a lot of our shareholders won't care. A lot don't because their purpose is to make money. But, many do. I love going on investor road trips.

You always get some who go beyond the numbers and want to talk to you about other things. This constituency isn't growing because there isn't yet enough evidence of companies doing this and being seen as successful. It's still too theoretical for them. But I don't see this as a problem. It's the right thing to do and people will see that."

This takes us right back to Desmond Tutu's statement on doing the right thing. Clearly that is emerging as a key operative term in deciphering what purpose is. We will come back to this later when we start understanding how we begin to craft purpose. For now, let's go back to ANZ and Elliott's purpose journey.

Elliott's very first visit as a CEO was to a branch in rural Australia. Elliott noticed that they had a sales board in the branch which showed targets for employees. When he asked how they managed to reconcile the publicly visible board with their promise of putting customers' needs first, the branch manager replied, "It's easy. Everyone knows me in this town. We live here." Elliott repeats the statement with emphasis: "We live here! That's what we have to get across to the public. We're still not seen as human, but we are. If all purpose does is capture this idea, then it's a good thing and is worth it."

There is a touch of irony in Elliott's statement when he says we are human, although we are not seen to be so. If any industry needs to rehumanize itself, it is the banking industry. And Elliott is adamant that ANZ does not fall into the metrics trap by 'dumbing down' purpose by turning it into a 'culture dashboard' that the regulators want to see. That is precisely why ANZ resisted going down to specific goals in the pursuit of purpose. Instead, Elliott says, "We're changing the mental model of banking and what it means to be a banker."

When we asked Elliott to describe further how purpose was helping ANZ take better decisions, he spoke of their diversity programme, their sponsorship of the Mardi Gras in Sydney for the LGBTIQ+ community and sponsoring refugees in jobs at the bank. Elliott went on to say that people did like those ideas in the past, but that until their purpose was articulated it was never clear *why* they did them.

From Banking to Helping Economic Participation

What purpose does is that it helps an organization build institutions. They invest in the future. ANZ's purpose, "shaping a world where people and communities thrive," as Elliott reminds us, "is to help economic participation". So ensuring diversity, LGBTIQ+ participation and refugee advancement are all manifestations of that purpose. Elliott says that employees can now say, "these programmes make sense to me, I now know what to do to support them." Purpose provides the *raison d'être* for why organizations do what they do and that is why it makes sense. Elliott isn't finished yet: "You know, right now, radicalization in migrant communities is a big deal in Australia. But radicalization is just a by-product of marginalization. We are about participation, which is an antidote to marginalization. Our refugee employees are some of the most amazing staff we have because they are so committed and that is because they are participating."

And that brings us to the very essence of why purpose is critical for ANZ. "Purpose makes sure that all of these efforts are coherent. That's the critical thing. Purpose gives us coherence."

Zopa: Banking for
the Gig Economy

"We wanted to make a difference; we wanted to make things better for people," says James Alexander when we met him after he had just spoken to a group of senior banking executives at a Duke CE leadership programme. The executives had left the room by now, confused and inspired by what they had just heard from James about Zopa.

James was one of the three people who created Zopa, the world's first peer-to-peer lending place where lenders and borrowers could meet to save and borrow money. "We have a choice and we can make up the rules." This is how Zopa was born in 2005. According to James, they didn't have the name until they had a desperate naming session where the team decided they would not leave the room until they had found a name. 'Zone of possible agreement' (Zopa) came from a negotiation class that James had taken at business school. They went online and bought the name from someone in Holland for $80. It was only later that they found out that it meant something entirely uncharitable in Russian.

Prior to Zopa, James had worked as a strategy director at EGG. He left EGG in 2003, along with a couple of colleagues, with one simple idea: to create a customer-centred business in finance. "We had no idea about what exactly we wanted to do, but we knew why we wanted to do this." Working with ethnographers and social economists, James and his colleagues had been able to piece together a perspective of what was emerging around them. They had identified a growing group of consumers that they had begun calling 'free-formers'. These were self-reliant people who 'had given up on the government' and were the forerunners to the current inhabitants of the gig economy.

James had realized that the free-formers were going to become the dominant demographic in the 21st century. These free-formers did want to invest their money, but not through the conventional channels that big banks were offering. When they were asked questions about borrowing they had a litany of complaints about the banking system. The many forms they were asked to fill, the sheer disdain the banks had for anyone who was self-reliant, or out of a job, or needed money for building an extension to their home. The biggest problem for the free-formers was that they felt disenfranchised by the banking system, as they were termed risky.

James and his colleagues went back to the very roots of banking and asked the disruptive question, "What if eBay lent money?" James himself had to borrow money from his father and jokes how he negotiated a better deal with his father than what his father was getting from one of the high street banks. Moreover, he could repay his father whenever he could and not be charged for it!

When they studied the writings of the economist Schumpeter, James and his colleagues began to understand how disruptive forces work. James remarked to us how surprised they were about the time it had taken big banks to see the disruption that was imminent. The industrial consumer age was giving way to the digital consumer age and the technology that could transform borrowing and lending was already there. As Thomas Paine said in 1776, "A long habit of not thinking a thing wrong gives it a superficial appearance of being right."

Zopa went on to win several awards, including the most trusted provider of great customer service. In 2015 they won the award for the most trusted loan provider and, in 2017, they were awarded a British bank award. They did things that no bank did and no bank could. They had open dis-cussion boards on their website where customers could post comments on what they liked and what they didn't. They went broke in the first year; the regulator tried to shut them down. "Innovation is messy," James keeps saying when he talks to audiences. "It is about seeing the world 'outside in' and making choices. Innovation is finding new and better ways to fulfil your organization's purpose."

Elliott's story at ANZ is about a 20th century institution going back to its purpose of serving the community amidst a broken global banking system in which people had lost trust with the industry. James's story at Zopa is about creating a new kind of bank for the 21st century with the question, 'What if eBay lent money?' Both stories demon-strate that the business opportunity for purpose shines bright and clear, be it a 184-year-old bank or a peer-to-peer lending institution.

CHAPTER 7

The Purpose of Purpose

"If we can really understand the problem, the answer will come out of it, because the answer is not separate from the problem."

J. KRISHNAMURTI

A Company for the Billions: Polman's Legacy

On a wintry February day in 2017, Paul Polman, the CEO of Unilever at that time, got the news. Kraft Heinz had made an audacious bid on the company he had led for the past nine years. No one had ever made a bid on Unilever and, in a turbulent environment with slowing growth, new competition from upstart brands and a deflation in developed markets, Unilever was suddenly looking vulnerable.

It had begun with Alexandre Behring, the chairman of Kraft Heinz calling on Paul Polman in the London headquarters of Unilever. Behring had asked Polman if he had ever considered a collaboration with Kraft Heinz, a rather innocuous way of starting a conversation. Then on 10 February, Behring returned to Unilever with a simple plan; it would acquire Unilever for $143 billion. This deal would have created the world's second largest consumer company by sales. For Kraft Heinz, it would have tripled the previous year's annual sales of $26.5 bn. From Dove soap to Ben and Jerry's ice cream, some of the most well-known global brands belonged to Unilever. Acquiring the company would mean a dominant grip not just in the US and Europe, but also in Asia. Kraft Heinz is controlled by Buffet's Berkshire Hathaway investment group and the Brazilian investor-led 3G Capital, known for their ruthless cost-cutting.

Paul Polman returned home that evening. He had already assembled a team to deal with the bid ever since Behring's first visit. In his mind, there was just no question of entertaining the offer, but the fact that Kraft Heinz could even contemplate it had shaken him to the core. That evening he had an epiphany and the words formed in his mind: "Unilever is a company for the billions and not for billionaires." His epiphany emerged from the very depths of his commitment not just to preserve Unilever, but what lay at the heart of Unilever: its very purpose. Like in the eighties when the Tylenol crisis shook Johnson & Johnson and James Burke had gone back to the J&J credo, a document that outlined the company's commitment to the needs and wellbeing of the people it served, Polman went right back to the reason for Unilever's existence.

A purposeful organization is one that devotes a considerable amount of its time and energy in defining and discussing why it exists, with a clear line of sight to its employees and all its stakeholders. And, as our research is telling us, in an increasingly disruptive 21st century, organizations need to spend a lot more time thinking about the reason why they exist and what they mean, not just for their customers and employees, but for all the stakeholders in their ecosystem. Purpose not only provides a place of calm in the turbulent waters of operating in complex systems, it also has a powerful business benefit, as we shall see.

For Polman, the bid was a clash between a long-term sustainable business model for multiple stakeholders that was at the heart of Unilever's purpose and a short-term one purely for the investors. In a world of unbridled capitalism and short-term maximization of profit, Polman has become something of a cult figure. For him, business has to be a part of the solution to the many challenges around us: inequality, poverty, unemployment and, of course, climate change. And he doesn't see sustainability through the conventional philanthropic lens of corporate and social responsibility either. There is a story going around in Unilever about the time when Polman was at a workshop when someone had drawn two circles on a flip chart, one circle denoting business and the other one sustainability. There was a small overlapping Venn space between the two circles standing for the proverbial sweet spot. Polman apparently walked up to the flip chart and tore up the paper, drew one large circle on a new sheet and wrote 'sustainable business' in large letters inside the circle.

Healing a Fractured World

At the 2018 World Economic Forum in Davos, the focus was on 'Strengthening Cooperation in a Fractured World' and Polman spoke eloquently about Unilever's commitment and efforts to close the gap on the 17 United Nation's goals for sustainable development. When he returned from Davos, he wrote a blog to all Unilever associates and began it with this: "In fact, to kick-start this year's meeting, Oxfam produced a report showing 82% of the wealth created last year went to the richest 1% and that 42 people today own the same amount as the poorest half of the rest of the world." Though not all CEOs feel comfortable in providing solutions, it did help to trigger a debate in Davos on how to bridge income inequality between the haves and the have-nots. Polman's message was simple and clear. He spoke passionately about changing food and land-use systems to ensure sustainable and nutritious food for everyone; more sustainable sourcing; equitable growth for all; and about the digital revolution and gender equality. In his blog, he suffixed each of the points he had made at Davos with the line "What this means to us" and outlined the further steps Unilever had to take as a company. As he always does, he squared back to the Unilever Sustainable Living Plan (USLP), with the line, "We now need to be sure that having taken the lead with the USLP, we continue to stay ahead and don't fall in love with our own pace of change, which increasingly risks being surpassed by others. Darwin after all was right – it is the most adaptable who survive."

Lopsided Logic

"Great companies identify something larger than transactions or business portfolios to provide purpose and meaning" wrote Rosabeth Moss Kanter in her 2011 HBR article on 'How Great Companies Think Differently'.[54] Great companies, according to Kanter, make choices about how to make money and they also think about building enduring institutions. In order to do so they invest in the future by thinking of investment holistically. We have great tools to define and measure economic logic, and business schools spend much of their time and energy in that. But we hardly spend any time on understanding what Kanter calls our institutional logic: the very reason for our existence.

Great companies focus on both business investment as well as relational investment in people and communities. In other words, truly great companies naturally see themselves as part of a sustainable ecosystem. In the 21st century, this becomes more crucial than anything else. With global information flows, digital technology and the advent of a new digital native who belongs to a world in which transparency and collaboration is the norm, the 21st century is disrupting the 20th century narrative of the sole purpose of business as making money from the environment. It is rapidly being replaced by a new reality of business ecosystems that operate on the basis of very different rules. These rules are significantly different from the ones that we have become accustomed to in the previous century.

To paraphrase Simon Sinek's notion of the golden circle, every company has an explanation for what they do, and some are pretty good at explaining how they do it. But very few are good at explaining why. Great companies, Sinek noticed, communicate from the inside out – from why to how to what – which is only possible when they have a powerful sense of purpose.

The Rise of Ecosystems

The term ecosystems originally came from biology and is attributed to British botanist Arthur Tansley who, in 1935, published this in the journal *Ecology*: "... although the organisms may claim our prime interest, when we are trying to think fundamentally, we cannot separate them from their special environments, with which they form one physical system."[55] Walk into the woods and you are surrounded by a magnificent ecosystem in which organisms, vegetation, plants and animals are in continuous interaction, linked together through energy flows and nutrient cycles. As mentioned earlier, the one principle that holds every ecosystem on the planet together: life creates life by sustaining conditions for life.

As such, ecosystems serve as a rich and evocative metaphor for the very purpose of life. "In nature, nothing exists alone" said the marine biologist and conservationist, Rachel Carson.[56] A decade later, scientist and thinker Gregory Bateson served a reminder by saying, "The major problems of the world are the result of the difference between how nature works and the way people think."[57] As we said earlier, nature thrives on complexity and its deep interconnections and interdependencies. In their book, *The Systems View of Life*,[58] authors Fritjof Capra and Pier Luigi Luisi discuss how nature must become a living metaphor for all human endeavour: "The 21st century zeitgeist is changing from one of world-as-machine to world-as-network."

Now some of you might be thinking, what is new about this? Virtually in all industries, organizations have always functioned in partnership with other players. Networks of suppliers, middlemen, retailers and ancillary industries are not new. But the logic was entirely different as it was based on the world-as-machine logic. This meant that the company or the factory came first as a unit and the relationships were the secondary modular parts. The ecosystem logic is exactly the opposite. The relationships are the unit! When Sony jettisoned using the MP3 format to which they had access, they did that on the basis of the world-as-machine logic. Seen from that perspective, the MP3 format represented a threat as it would cannibalize the old business model which Sony's music industry thrived in. What they saw as a threat, Apple saw as an opportunity. Steve Jobs saw a community in which Apple would be a dynamic and co-evolving actor, creating value through collaboration.

Working within ecosystems also provides businesses with a competitive advantage. Nokia failed to realize this until it was too late, and kept beavering away at developing its own operating system Symbian, while a new ecosystem was emerging around it. By the time it decided to abandon Symbian and adopt Android, it was woefully too late.

Ecosystems also serve another important purpose: they change the frame through which you perceive the other players in the network. Customers, suppliers and every stakeholder, including non-governmental organizations (NGOs), are not passive recipients but active collaborators shaping the evolution of the system as a whole. A great example of such an evolution is the way in which LEGO has moved away from selling toy bricks to a very specific customer base to becoming an ecosystem player. The inspiration it needed for its blockbuster movie, *The Lego Movie*, came from YouTube, which was the platform for a bunch of top-motion films that were using LEGO bricks!

Institutional Logic

We want to take the notion of ecosystems a step further and propose the following:

A. Organizations that do not recreate themselves to operate as members of an ecosystem are in all likelihood making themselves irrelevant

B. Ecosystems are the 21st century networks through which organizations can build enduring value and meaning

Let us get back to Rosabeth Kanter and correct the lopsided logic that she refers to. According to Kanter, the secret behind the practices of great companies like Unilever is that they are not solely defined by their economic logic. They also build a social or institutional logic. Institutional logic, according to Kanter, holds that "companies ... are also vehicles for accomplishing societal purposes and for providing meaningful livelihoods for those who work in them". So the value a company creates is measured not just in terms of its short-term profits, but how it sustains the conditions with people and society that allow it to flourish over time.

Is this a wildly new idea? Not at all, considering that our natural ecosystems have behaved this way for millions of years. As we've said many times before in this book, life creates conditions for life and that is an apt description of this logic. If nature began using the model of maximizing short-term profits at the expense of long-term sustainability, our life support systems would simply come to a rapid halt.

Building Social Institutions

Kanter also goes on to point out that this was hardly a new idea before business became committed to the myth of shareholder value as its sole driving force. There are numerous examples of industrialists who have founded successful institutions in the past. The story of Unilever is one such story. In the 1890s, William Hesketh Lever, founder of Lever Brothers, wrote down his ideas for Sunlight Soap – his revolutionary new product that helped popularize cleanliness and hygiene in Victorian England. It was "to make cleanliness commonplace; to lessen work for women; to foster health and contribute to personal attractiveness, that life may be more enjoyable and rewarding for the people who use our products".[59]

"The [purpose] of Lord Lever when he made his Sunlight bar soap was to address the issues of hygiene in Victorian Britain," states Paul Polman. "The reason I believe business should be around is to serve society," he adds. That sense of purpose has remained a part of Unilever's culture and has now morphed into "making sustainable living commonplace". When Polman became the CEO in 2009, he spent a night in Lever's bed on top of the roof to immerse himself into Lever's legacy. The USLP that is known in every corner of Unilever offices and factories worldwide probably came out of that night on the roof. [60]

Polman echoes Kanter's view that only when leaders think of themselves as builders of social institutions can their organizations master changes and challenges. Especially in an accelerating 21st century, this becomes a critical requirement. While economic logic drives shareholder value, it is institutional logic that "serves as a buffer against uncertainty and change by providing corporations with a coherent identity".[61]

When we asked Polman to describe how he went about defending Unilever from the Kraft Heinz takeover, his reply was that he was confident that he would have the support of his shareholders, the charity workers and the trade unions. A YouGov petition with 100,000 signatures was kept ready. Companies like Unilever build social equity, not just with customers but also with a wide range of stakeholders. And, interestingly, they can even have the support of the shareholders, as in the case of Unilever.

How do companies like Unilever create institutional logic? They use societal values and their purpose as decision-making criteria. This means defining the very identity of a business in terms of its purpose and ensuring that everything else becomes a manifestation of that purpose. The USLP that was launched in 2010 includes environmental factors,

improving conditions for customers and workers, inno-
vating new products that are environmentally and socially
sustainable and nudging suppliers and collaborators to act
in the same way. Polman believes that in the 21st century
these are not just good things to do, but in the gig economy
they provide a 'license to operate' as public scrutiny becomes
ubiquitous thanks to social media. As part of the USLP, the
company is collaborating with NGOs like the Rainforest
Alliance to improve farming practices. Nine years later,
Unilever continues to stick to the USLP with a fierce and
unwavering commitment.

Intangible Assets: Building Institutional Logic with Sustainable Brands

According to Alex Edmans, professor of finance at the London Business School, the most important assets in a 21st
century firm are intangible. These include the company's
corporate culture, its innovative capability and its environmental sustainability. For that reason, purpose becomes
the intrinsic locus from where decisions get taken, whether
to use technology to transform customer's lives for better,
or to preserve the environment for future generations. As
Edmans writes, profits are the "extrinsic goal", but purposeful companies "will make an investment simply because it
is the right thing to do ..."[62]

Does purpose pay? Edmans cites compelling evidence
that purpose is critical for a firm's long-term success. "In
particular, purpose glues the different stakeholders of an
organization – customers, employees, suppliers, communities and investors – towards a common mission." For
instance, Edmans uses 26 years of data to demonstrate that

"the ethical treatment of workers is associated with 2–3% higher stock returns every year."

Keith Weed, who recently retired as head of marketing for Unilever would speak animatedly about the USLP that would enable the company to source 100% of its raw material sustainably by 2020. Recently named the world's most influential CMO, Weed talks animatedly about how consumers are increasingly looking for – and expecting to see – the purpose behind the brand. "Brand purpose gives people a constant in a constantly changing world."[63] Outlining Unilever's vision for making sustainable living commonplace, Weed made the case by saying that Unilever's sustainable brands were growing at twice the rate of the rest of its portfolio and delivering more than half its growth.

Weed mentions Unilever's membership in Collectively.org, a social platform that encourages people to take meaningful action in a positive way. "It is about making choices that are better for them and for the planet and to demand solutions that make the world a healthier, happier place." He refers to brands as citizens who have a responsibility to create and lead positive change in an increasingly complex and hyper-connected world.

It is not just brands; there is a process of innovation at Unilever that is made possible because of its purpose. In developing and emerging countries where water is scarce, around 40% of domestic water is used to wash clothes, a task which is done by hand. Rinsing uses around 70% of this water, with the removal of soap suds being a large contributor to the rinsing process. Consumers keep rinsing until there are no visible soap suds left. To reduce the volume of water used during rinsing, Unilever developed a new anti-foam molecule that breaks down soap suds more quickly. This reduces the amount of water needed, as well as speeding up the process of rinsing. Unilever's commitment to help consumers save water enabled it to develop a product called SmartFoam. SmartFoam, a patented technology for Unilever, is a direct result from shared clarity of purpose.

In 2016, the company launched its Sunlight 2-in-1 hand washing laundry powder with SmartFoam technology in South Africa, which had been experiencing its worst drought in over 30 years. As part of their work in South Africa, they installed 250 push taps in the Johannesburg community of Tembisa and ran a campaign to raise awareness and educate residents on how they could save water. They also launched SmartFoam technology in India, another country experiencing severe drought.

Another example of Unilever's commitment to USLP is the Comfort One Rinse product that cuts water use in laundry. This fabric conditioner reduces the amount of water needed to rinse to one bucket rather than three, thereby halving the volume of water needed per wash – around 30 litres – amounting to over 500 billion litres of water saved every year.

In 2016, with Vietnam enduring its worst drought in 90 years, in partnership with government authorities Unilever launched the 'Rinse once to donate clean water to help Vietnam' campaign. Through purchasing Comfort One Rinse, consumers could both reduce their own water use and donate water to rural communities in the ten regions most impacted by the drought.

Within two months, 111,000 m^3 of water had been donated and two water pipelines – to bring clean water into rural villagers' homes – were being constructed. Additionally, 510 water tanks were provided so rural communities could store clean water. The campaign reached around

17 million consumers through television and over 7 million through Facebook. During the campaign, sales of Comfort One Rinse grew by 27%, compared to the average market growth of 2% over the same period, reinforcing our view that sustainability is good for business.

Leadership with Purpose

As this book goes into press, companies like Unilever are facing increasing challenges in an accelerating environment. The age of the 20th century multinational is being disrupted as local competitors and innovative business models develop new ways of positioning brands and customer offerings. FMCG companies like Unilever need to learn quickly to adapt to a very different environment from what they are used to. The fast-moving phrase does not just apply to consumer goods, but equally well to the 21st century consumer. How does Unilever remain relevant in a new world in which a smartbot, Alexa, is helping consumers make choices?

A recent *Bloomberg* article, aptly titled 'If Unilever Can't Make Feel-Good Capitalism Work, Who Can?',[64] asks the all-important question about how long idealism can survive. Buckley and Campbell, the authors of the article, write about how Unilever is the first company to attempt 'making the world a better place' mantra on the 'greatest of industrial scales'. The question is, as they ask, can Unilever continue to fight some fundamental laws of the financial system and continue to make conscientious capitalism work. In other words, is there still room enough for institutional logic in a world that is being dislocated by digital technology?

Our argument is that it is probably more relevant than ever before. Purpose is much more than just idealism: it is an intelligent response that is at once pragmatic and inspiring.

The world in which we live, work and lead is becoming increasingly interconnected, interdependent and complex, and in this new emergent scenario the old ways of doing business are starting to come apart.

Purpose is not about feel-good capitalism; it is becoming a dominant source of competitive advantage. As information becomes a commodity and digital technology shifts the economy from assets to access, purpose becomes the key that enables organizations to engage with customers and stakeholders on whom they rely for their very survival.

In a 2018 talk to some senior general managers at Four Acres, Polman spoke evocatively of why purpose provides a powerful resource to leaders and organizations. He spoke of liberty and responsibility, the two sides of purpose in an almost Janus-like depiction of the term. Purpose provides the liberty to imagine the world as a better place and work hard towards it, but it also reminds us of our great responsibility. Purpose, then, is a choice we make. And purpose inspires great leadership.

As this book goes into print, after a decade of being at the helm, Polman has announced his retirement and his worthy successor, Alan Jope, has stepped into the role. In a farewell address to the general manager community in Unilever, Polman gave his humanizing message to this group one last time: "You have to be a real person in the real world. Otherwise you cannot run a business. Take care of purpose, people and values and the rest will come." He suddenly stopped and asked the audience what big event they could recall having happened the previous day. Someone in the audience referred to an event in the Netherlands. "Four people dying in the Netherlands makes news, but 400 people dying in Mozambique does not," replied Polman. Then he paused and asked what Unilever has heard him ask so many times,

"Do you really care?" He ended his talk with these lines: "As leaders, we have to be good human beings. Purpose for me comes from three things: dignity of all people, equity in society and compassion for all. Your job is to live your purpose and unleash energy in others."

Perhaps the most appropriate tribute to Polman comes from Richard Edelman, who wrote this in an article aptly titled, "Paul Polman – The CEO Who Changed Capitalism": "... his most significant achievement has been to inspire fellow CEOs to look beyond financial results, to address the world's pressing societal issues."[65]

CHAPTER 8

Purpose and Empathy Come before Strategy

"To know what one ought to do is certainly the hardest thing in life. 'Doing' is comparatively easy."

MARIA MITCHELL

The Missing Question

At this stage in our discussion, it's important to situate purpose in terms of our organizational structures and capabilities. As a starting point, it's helpful to look through the lens of the dominant silos or functions and enquire what fundamental questions people in those silos hold in their minds explicitly or implicitly every day.

Take marketing. Their dominant questions correspond to the four Ps of marketing (product, price, promotion and place): 'What?' 'How Much?' 'How?' and 'Where?'. Then there's finance: 'How much?' (income statement) and 'When?' (balance sheet/time value of money). Of course, let's not forget R&D: 'What?' and 'How?'. Human resources? You guessed it: 'Who?' (people and talent), 'How?' (development) and 'How much?' (compensation and benefits).

Purpose is like the source of a river, continually bubbling away and giving birth to the river of values. 'What do we fundamentally care about?' 'How should we behave?' These are values questions. And as the river flows down through the valleys, it becomes the vision: 'What does success look like?' And, finally, as the river meanders through the plains and diverges into multiple streams and rivulets, comes the strategy question: 'What choices must we make?'

Our focus in this book is in that place in the mountains where the river is being continuously born: Why does it matter?

Leaders own Four Questions

Think of it this way; as a leader you own four fundamental questions about your organization.

The Purpose Question:	Why do we uniquely exist?
The Values Question:	What do we fundamentally care about? How should we behave?
The Vision Question:	What does success look like?
The Strategy Question:	What choices must we make?

As you can see there is a pecking order here. Think again of the metaphor of a river; the generative source is purpose, without it there is no river.

So, what does Purpose actually do?

Packard's words, "Why are we here?" continue to be powerful, decades afterwards. Shayne Elliott referred to it as doing the right thing, Polman called it caring and, as we move through this book, we will have other voices bringing in other nuances to this word, purpose. For now, we can create a conceptual framework for purpose by stating what it does:

1. States why you exist, what you exist to do or be, and your reason for being
2. Clarifies the unique value that you bring
3. Articulates what need you are filling that is unique to you
4. States what you are 'called' upon to do
5. Defines the boundaries of your playing field; what work or business you choose to be in
6. Can describe whom you serve
7. Can articulate what is unique about your methods
8. Represents that part of your company's (group's or team's) essence that is always true, regardless of any particular vision for the future

It allows you to do the right thing

In September 1982, several people in Chicago died from taking extra-strength Tylenol that had been deliberately laced with potassium cyanide, a deadly poison. The manufacturers, Johnson & Johnson, withdrew every product from every shelf in the US and stopped its production. The contamination did not happen in their plant, but J&J took complete responsibility for it. James Burke, the CEO, was asked later how he coped with the enormously difficult situation of withdrawing products knowing that the share price would plummet right away. His reply was simple: "It was the right thing to do."

The right action, the defining characteristic of good leadership emerges out of purpose, which asks the question, 'Why do we exist uniquely in this world?' This question assumes critical importance during a crisis, as Burke's example shows. Leaders who operate effectively in crises are 'merchants of meaning', fluent in navigating complexity, because they have a clear line of sight with the larger purpose that is guiding them through the chaos and uncertainty.

Leaders like Burke understand complexity. They know that it plays out in unpredictable and differentiated ways, but it is held together by principles of integration. These principles are usually obscure because it requires a higher cognitive level to see them. Rather than waste energy and resources in trying to control the differentiation, they focus their attention on stepping back and discovering the integrating principle, what we the authors refer to as 'the signal in the noise'.

Burke's question to his team was, "What is the most ethical thing we can now do as a company, given our focus on the safety of customers and patients?" He did not ask about the shareholder value proposition. The story goes that one of Burke's senior team members had been on the phone with the lawyers who were of the opinion that as the contamination had not happened in the plant J&J was absolved of all blame. Burke's stand was that no matter where the contamination took place, Tylenol was J&J's product and, as such, they would take all responsibility.

It helps you define your boundaries

In Belgium in the late nineties a batch of Coca-Cola had a problem with the flavour because something had gone wrong with the mix during the filling process in the factory. It tasted of sulfur and several children who had consumed the drink had gone to hospital. Now remember that Coca-Cola's stated purpose at that time was to increase shareholder value. As a result, the company quickly sorted out the technical side of the problem and said it was an off-mix issue and not toxic. That's it; nothing more was said, no recall, nothing, and no further action taken.

As we wrote earlier, purpose states why a company exists, the very reason for its being. And it clarifies the value your company adds to customers, people and society. But also, and importantly, purpose fulfils the giant task of defining the boundaries of your playing field. Coca-Cola could achieve none of this at that time. As a result, the company missed out on an important opportunity to explore and deepen its relationship with the society that it was serving. On a humorous twist to the tale, more children began turning up at local hospitals over the next few days as it turned out that they had found a convenient way of getting out of school! The end result was very different from J&J's story. The Belgian Health Ministry eventually forced Coca-Cola to withdraw all its products from shelves across the country, at a huge economic cost and a hit to its corporate reputation and brand.

Check the difference between these statements coming from two sets of senior managers from two car companies when asked a simple question: 'What business are you in?' The first group of managers from company A said, "We are in the business of making and selling cars", while the other group from company B pondered over the question and said, "We are in the business of enhancing human transportation". Both companies are well-known brands, but which one of the two had a better perspective on their playing fields? That perspective provides for innovation and the ability to adapt with agility to changes in the environment. Because of a much wider and deeper perspective, company B may even stop making cars and find novel ways of enhancing how we move from one place to another. Incidentally, company A was Chrysler and company B was Honda.

It opens up future evolutionary pathways

Purpose is not transient and it is not meant to change. It carries the story of the organization forward. It evolves and adapts as an unfolding story does, but it does not fundamentally change. We are often asked about the relationship between purpose and vision, as they sound a lot alike. Then there is the typical garbled usage of vision and mission in the same breath as 'we're doing the vision-mission thing at an offsite' that we hear so many times. It is usually accompanied by the sentiment of 'let's get this done quickly so that we can get into the more important stuff like strategy.'

There are two levels of meaning that need to be spelled out here: vision is something that expires. For example, you may have a vision that takes you to 2025, and then when you pass it you have to set a new one. Purpose is the thing that endures over time. Like standing over a globe, you may not see what follows the 2025 vision because of the curve in the horizon, but purpose is that clear line that allows you to navigate the curve despite not being able to see the horizon after 2025. That is precisely what enables the members of an organization to have ongoing conversations about purpose and to shape its evolution.

International healthcare company BUPA holds a purpose that is simple and clear: 'Longer, Healthier, Happier Lives'. This purpose resonantly remains at the heart of everything that BUPA does. "We talk about it all the time and it's always what drives what we do, both internally and externally," an employee told us. Once again, it provides perspective, is energizing and strong and, most importantly, it sets wide boundaries.

When the NHS was started in the UK in 1948, it began with a similar proposition based on three simple principles:

that it meet the needs of everyone, that it be free at the point of delivery and that it be based on clinical need, not ability to pay. However, if you look at the purpose of the NHS today, it appears in the form of a wordy and wooly 'constitution' running over several pages and with seven guiding principles. It reads as if it was put together either by a committee or by a PR consulting firm. While the comparison between a private insurance firm like BUPA and the NHS may be unfair because of their respective scales and resources, the point is that the power of purpose applies equally to the private and public sectors. The NHS displays typical problems that organizations face when they have shut off pathways of evolution as a result of an inarticulate purpose. Lots of change management programmes that do not yield any significant change. More noise, less signal. The core question to ask is, 'Is your purpose keeping evolutionary pathways open?'

How does purpose become the driving force?

As mentioned earlier, we met Denise Pickett, President of American Express's US consumer services division, and asked about what it takes to make purpose work as a motivating force. Pickett focused on the importance of embedding purpose across the organization: "Purpose won't work unless it's 'institutionalized': everyone from the guy in the post room to the Chief Executive must buy into it and live it." Pickett contrasted this with strategy by adding, "Strategy is always chunked down and changed to target different levels of the business. It will never be digestible for everyone all together – so it cannot be a guiding light for 10,000 people."

As a Canadian, she explained that purpose is like the (modern, constitutional) monarchy that, when functioning properly, unites people around a singular idea, "Whereas strategy is like complex, hard-to-understand government. Great strategy is like good government. It's crucial – but it doesn't excite people," she said. Pickett found applying the purpose of her division – 'creating extraordinary customer experiences every day, everywhere' – brought her closer to customers: an exercise of real value for leaders who can otherwise drift away from the very people they are supposed to serve.

"As you get more senior, the distance between you and the customer gets bigger – when it should get closer," she admits. "But when I was Canada country manager, I'd apply our purpose and for a day every couple of weeks I'd get out there and just talk to customers. It energized me. Your people have to be convinced that it's not just a tagline – it's real." This is what Pickett means by institutionalization – the organization and everyone within it should embody the purpose of the organization. What Pickett terms 'excavation'– talking to the people within and without the organization to garner insights – is key to starting the process.

"When I came to run the US consumer business, it took six months," she reveals. "We talked to customers and employees, we pressure-tested ideas. I didn't want to come in and say 'this is it'. That wouldn't have been genuine." This focus on employee and customer priorities could appear to clash with those of shareholders. Yet, on this topic, Pickett is resolute. "I tend to focus on the customer and the employee. And the customer is always at the centre for me. I don't really put it through a shareholder lens. Purpose is a long-term investment and that's where you get the alignment with shareholder interest. The outcome is better for shareholders, but it's not the starting point or rallying point.

Shareholders are not the guiding light. If you put the employee engagement first and then keep customers at the centre, shareholder returns will follow."

Perhaps that is Pickett's greatest insight; if you lead your people from a clear sense of purpose, profits will naturally follow. In her, American Express has a prescient thinker. Purpose matters because, when done right, it drives employee engagement as well as customer focus: not only a winning formula, but also a formula for winning.

Purpose as a Living Force

The Shrikhande Clinic is a hospital in Dadar, a leafy suburb of Mumbai. Named after Dr V.N. Shrikhande, who continues to practise at the age of 87, the hospital is spread over four floors. Unlike most other hospitals in India, this one stands out because it does not feel like a hospital. First of all, everyone you meet – from the receptionist to the cleaner – greets you with a smile. It is spotlessly clean and has the ambience of a retreat more than anything else. But the most notable part of this hospital is the attention that you receive from the doctors. Dr Nande, a surgeon at the hospital, who was once Dr Shrikhande's student and is now his son-in-law, exudes the quality of attention with the patients. "No question is too much," he says gently, knowing that much of the healing process lies in the doctor's conversation with the patient.

Unhurried and with uncharacteristic warmth, the doctors display a level of empathy and caring that is rare, especially in the hurly burly of Mumbai's medical practice. This place is clearly special. Dr Shrikhande was telling us about the time they built the hospital and the builders kept asking why he wanted the patient rooms to be this big. Typical of the real estate mania in a city choking with buildings, every square foot is an opportunity to make more money. "Pointing to the trees outside the windows and the new spring blossoms on them," Dr Shrikhande said, "what the patient looks out on is a part of the healing process".

In 1994, Dr Shrikhande was invited to operate on the then President of India, Dr Shankar Dayal Sharma. In view of the president's advanced age and complicated massive hernia, he was advised to go abroad for surgery. Several surgeons who had examined the president had advocated that the risks of operating were too high. The president's systemic illnesses meant that general anaesthesia was not possible and all the other surgeons had ruled out any attempts at operating with local anaesthesia. Dr Shrikhande operated on him successfully at the Army Hospital in New Delhi under local anaesthesia, even if "the night before (the operation) was not without its jitters," he says with a characteristic twinkle in his eye.

Notwithstanding his great operating skills, what stands out about Dr Shrikhande is his sensitivity towards patients and their illnesses. Clearly, here is someone who has never lost his sense of purpose. In his book, *Reflections of a Surgeon*,[66] he writes about his time as a student in the dissection hall of the Grant Medical College. "The sight of the cadavers would trigger a chain of thought. Where was he born? How did he live? They had died unheard, unsung and unwept. What must have been the dreams of their parents? Did they go to school? How much did they suffer?"

In a chapter titled, *Courage in the face of death*, he talks about Keroba, a poor man rendered paraplegic by a car accident, and about two other patients who were dying. "My patients have taught me how to live, why to live and also how to die ... one life is enough for me. I have enjoyed my long life that took me to unknown heights and remain grateful."

In our research, we have found that situating purpose in the organization involves fundamentally looking at the meaning it is meant to impart. The underlying thinking and assumptions we make about purpose matter in order for it to deliver the perspective and clarity that we have been discussing.

A One-way Ticket to Mars

Adriana Marais is one of 100 people on the shortlist to go on a one-way trip to Mars. If you haven't heard of her, that might be because the launch is still a way off. The Mars One project expects to send its first four settlers to the Red Planet by the early 2030s. Marais, along with 99 others, have beaten out over 200,000 other applicants to compete for four places.

Mars One was founded in 2011 by Arno Wielders and Bas Lansdorp. The venture rests on two fascinatingly easy-to-conceive assumptions. First, we are just about at the point in our development as a species where such a mission is technically feasible. And, the entire mission can be self-referentially funded by the proceeds from a documentary that will chronicle the mission. The first launch, estimated to cost $10bn seems readily attainable when one looks at the fact that the London Olympics generated over $8bn in advertising revenue over a relatively short period.

Marais, an accomplished South African physicist, spoke about her mission at Duke CE's conference 'The Human Difference: Leading in a Digital Age', in August 2017 in Johannesburg, South Africa. "I have learned that purpose is all about perspective: that is, a sense of that which is enduring and systemic and entirely beyond the financial or strategic."

We found Marais' perspective, in terms of time horizon and altitude – literally and figuratively – unsurpassed in our conversations about purpose thus far. After all, if you're going to Mars and never coming back to Earth, your sense of purpose must be profound.

In our conversation with Adriana Marais, we found that there were three core ideas that underpinned her sense of purpose and, like any good scientist, she did not dwell on arcane or quasi-spiritual concepts, but stuck with scientific facts.

1. There is no 'individual'; Purpose is inherently collective

Marais remembers becoming aware at an early age of the fact that there is no such thing, scientifically speaking, as a single living organism, living in isolation. "From our parents to the bacteria in our gut to the food we eat, we see clear evidence that we as humans instead should be thought of as part of a living network." Challenging the dominant world-view of the individual as the unit of existence, Marais goes on to assert, "In fact, it is this network that allows us to be alive at all. Even the oxygen we breathe is due to the oxygenic extinction event that occurred on the Earth about two billion years ago, so multi-cellular life owes its very existence to its bacterial predecessors, all of which are gone."

The implications are profound. It means that if we cannot conceive of our existence as isolated then, by definition, we cannot see our purpose as located in the individual unit. Instead, 'individual' purpose must necessarily be intertwined with the purpose of our organizations and institutions which, in turn, are intertwined with larger institutions and networks.

2. Curiosity and learning are innately human and purposeful

"We physicists are devoted to discovering the blocks of reality." Marais stresses on how the joy of discovery is the real purpose behind doing science. "What could be more amazing than uncovering new knowledge at a vastly accelerated rate that being the first humans on another planet will afford us?" Curiosity is human and innately purposeful and no artificial intelligence (AI) can replicate that. To rehumanize leadership and to live from purpose is to bring back curiosity in everything we do.

3. Purpose requires looking through the lens of legacy and stewardship

"Humans are unique in their ability to generate and pass on new knowledge. We are not the first species to change the climate on a global scale and cause the extinction of other species, but we are probably the first to be aware of it," says Marais. "My sense of purpose has a more collective focus as well as the selfish: by going to Mars, we will be making an unprecedented contribution to human knowledge. We'll learn more about water recycling, food production and sustainability in the microcosm of our settlement than we could learn in several lifetimes." Marais is convinced that when this knowledge is shared, it will help our species develop the technologies to extend our collective survival. And then Marais went on to talk about something startling, a thought that had been lingering at the back of our minds: the prospect of mission failure. Her sense of purpose and perspective was unshaken. "Even if we die on impact, the knowledge and learning that would come from that impact event would be more than what I could ever produce on Earth."

We did ask Marais about the challenge to this mission that would inevitably arise from sceptics. "Sure, lots of people are saying we have bigger problems on Earth. Why not devote a mission to those issues?" She answers her own question by saying, "However, I believe that there is something about getting some 'fresh air' (not literally!) to change your perspective. A mission to another planet gets us out of our default thinking. Earth's ideology is very crowded and it's hard to see that when you're surrounded by entrenched ideas. On Mars we can start fresh and think about new ways of living and even thriving."

The conversation with Marais revealed how purpose is at once individual and collective, almost like two sides of the same coin. Or more like the yin-yang description in Chinese philosophy. Organizational purpose must be able to resonate at a collective level, as in Unilever's sustainability agenda or ANZ's economic participation, but it must also be felt at an individual level by everyone working inside these organizations.

We also learned that purpose has to be, in one form or another, about the service of others and about exploration and learning that naturally flows from that sense of service. We had never thought that curiosity would be such an important feature of purpose, but Marais helped us see that. But most of all, Marais' message was that purpose must come from a new perspective and a fresh point of view. We will not be going to Mars, but we feel that our dialogue helped us see that the purpose of purpose is to take us where no one has gone before. Game on!

CHAPTER 9

The Empathic Leader

"I've learned that people will forget what you said, people will forget what you did, but people will never forget how you made them feel."

MAYA ANGELOU

In 1992, Giacomo Rizzolatti, a neuroscientist at the University of Parma, was experimenting with his team of researchers who were recording electrical activity from neurons in the brain of a macaque monkey. Tiny electrodes were inserted into the brains of the macaque monkeys. Rizolatti and his team were studying the neurons that fired when the monkey moved its arm to grab an object. The story goes that the research team forgot to turn off their equipment when they went to get their lunch.

A totally serendipitous discovery was to follow. A graduate student was eating an ice cream cone in full view of the monkey in the experiment. To the surprise of the team, the electrodes suddenly began to signal a spike in cellular activity in the premotor cortex, even though the monkey was not performing any movements. This meant that the neurons in the monkey's brain were mirroring the actions of the researchers.

Rizolatti went on to call these 'mirror neurons', as they seemed to perform the task of simulating neural activity as if the monkey was performing the action itself.

Since that serendipitous discovery, many experiments have been carried out and an experiment in 2016 on the response of single neurons in human beings brought clear evidence that we display similar patterns. According to Rizzolatti, "Mirror neurons allow us to grasp the minds of others not through conceptual reasoning but through direct simulation."

Mirror neurons went on to be known as 'empathy neurons' suggesting that we might be more hardwired for empathy than previously thought. A sudden spate of research into empathy is starting to throw out some very interesting results. School assessments are starting to measure empathy as a competency; so is leadership development.

Mirroring Each Other

Mirror neurons are a particular type of neurons that fire not only when you perform a certain action, but also when you see someone else doing the same thing, even if you're not doing it yourself. Rizzolatti's discovery suggests that our brains work not only via logical interpretation, but also by feeling. Humans physically express feelings through gestures, facial expressions, etc.

Marco Iacoboni, is Professor of Psychiatry and Bio-behavioural Sciences and Director of the Marco Iacoboni Lab, UCLA Brain Mapping Centre at the University of California, Los Angeles. He is the author of *Mirroring People: The Science of Empathy and How we Connect with Others*.[67] In an interview with Jonah Lehrer, *Mind Matters* editor for *Scientific American*, Iacoboni said: "Mirror neurons are the only brain cells we know of that seem specialized to code the actions of other people and also our own actions ... When I see you smiling, my mirror neurons for smiling fire up too, initiating a cascade of neural activity that evokes the feeling we typically associate with a smile. I don't need to make any inference on what you are feeling, I experience immediately and effortlessly (in a milder form, of course) what you are experiencing."[68]

Iacoboni goes on to point out that our minds connect when our bodies mirror each other; that is a fundamental phenomenon for empathy. But how do we build a culture of empathy? Iacoboni replies: "Evolution has placed in our brains a system – a relatively simple system – that makes us wired for empathy. We have been taught for centuries that we are selfish beings preoccupied with maximizing profits for ourselves, that's the traditional teaching of human nature. It is wrong. We have a natural predisposition for being empathic." Iacoboni is only reinforcing what we said in the prologue and in Chapter 1: that the dominant narrative of self-maximization at the expense of everything else has shaped our mindsets and behaviours.

The good news is that emotions are contagious and we can create a virtuous cycle. The only way to intervene in making people more empathic is to get yourself into the mind of the other person; only then can you have a meaningful interaction with the other person. To see the point of view of the other person.

Building Empathy

Iacoboni is of the opinion that attacks on empathy are a reaction to the traditional notion being challenged that human beings are selfish and self-maximizing. The people who support that view feel threatened. But can empathy be built?

"Imitation is a great way of becoming empathic. Let's throw away our beliefs as they come in the way of empathy; we have to see the humanity of others, even people you disagree with."

Iacoboni is taking us straight into the topic of rehumanization. "Beliefs are blinders. They create social groups and you have to belong to a group so you identify with the group. You become very empathic with the members of your group but you are every unempathic with members of the other group. Let's start with a fundamental fact: we are all human."

As we wrote in the prologue to this book, empathy is the second humanizing vector of evolution. It is likely to have developed from the need to deal with a hostile environment and to interact and communicate with large groups. The need to belong was the driving force.

In *The Empathic Civilization*,[69] Jeremy Rifkin wrote, "Empathy conjures up active engagement: the willingness of an observer to become part of another's experience, to share the feeling of that experience." Empathy, according to Rifkin, lies at the very core of human existence. His conclusion is that "we are soft-wired not for aggression, violence, self-interest and utilitarianism," but rather "for sociability, attachment, affection and companionship."

Backing up his work with scientific data, Rifkin contends that "the empathic evolution of the human race and the profound ways it has shaped our development and will likely decide our fate as a species." 'Homo empathicus', as Rifkin terms the human race, is "a fundamentally empathetic species" and writes that the progress of civilization has been a perpetual struggle between "empathy and entropy". While empathy is about human connection, entropy is driving the deterioration of the planet. What Rifkin means is that as civilizations get increasingly more complex, the more communication we get. However, civilizations also consume more energy at alarming rates as they get more complex. What is required, writes Rifkin, is "nothing less than a leap to global empathic consciousness and in less than a generation if we are to resurrect the global economy and revitalize the biosphere."

Rifkin is optimistic that "the empathic civilization is emerging. A younger generation is fast extending its empathic embrace beyond religious affiliations and national identification to include the whole of humanity and the vast project of life that envelops the Earth."

Is Empathy Hardwired?
The Neuroscience of Empathy

The Association for Psychological Science organized a symposium on the neuroscience of empathy in 2017, as part of the International Convention for Psychological Science in Vienna. Christian Keysers of the Netherlands Institute for Neuroscience has been doing work on whether the motor mirroring system that we carry in us as human beings helps us to understand the inner states behind the actions of others. "When we witness what happens to others, we don't just activate the visual cortex, like we thought some decades ago. We also activate our own actions as if we'd be acting in similar ways. We activate our own emotions and sensations as if we felt the same."[70]

However, empathy is not as globally responsive as research has shown. Our brains may allow us to feel empathy for another's experiences, but they are not necessarily great at bridging the cross-cultural divide, or the divide with anyone who happens to be different. The distinction between what psychologists call in-group and out-group members continues to play its role. This remains a barrier to empathy. The question is, how can we overcome it?

Collaboration as a Competitive Advantage

Greg Satell is an author, speaker and innovation advisor who runs a blog called Digital Tonto. In one of his blogs he uses the example of Linus Torvalds releasing the Linux kernel on the internet, inviting others to download, use and modify it. A community was created in a very short amount of time and, as Satell says, their "contributions transformed it into an operating system that rivalled those of even corporate giants like Microsoft." Satell thinks that we are just about starting to scratch the surface of open source: "In fact, as our ability to connect to ecosystems of talent, technology and information continues to increase exponentially, the solution to many tough problems is becoming more social than technical.

"The truth is that today the possibilities of many technologies far exceed the ability of any one firm to capitalize on them. So the key to competitive advantage is no longer to optimize value chains, but to extend capabilities through collaboration, either directly or through platforms. In a networked world, the best way to become a dominant player is to be an indispensable partner."

In his book, *Humans are Underrated*,[71] Geoff Colvin, editor-at-large at *Fortune* magazine, paints a picture of how robotics and AI are transforming the world. Colvin challenges the picture we might be holding on to that the highest skilled jobs will still be done by human beings, say, a surgeon. He writes of how researchers at the UC Berkeley are training a robot to 'identify and cut away cancerous tissue' entirely on its own.

So how do humans add value? Our mistake, according to Colvin, is that we keep thinking there are skills that computers will not acquire, but we keep being wrong about the predictions. What we need to do is ask, what are humans most driven to do?

At one time we felt that driving a vehicle required split second judgments and, as such, only humans could do it, and we were wrong. Yes, figuring out what computers will never do is an exceedingly perilous route to determining how humans can remain valuable. A better strategy is to ask, what are the activities that we humans, driven by our deepest nature or by the realities of daily life, will simply insist be performed by other humans, even if computers could do them?

"We want to follow human leaders, even if a computer could say all the right words, which is not an implausible prospect. We want to hear our diagnosis from a doctor, even if a computer supplied it, because we want to talk to the doctor about it – perhaps just to talk and know we're being heard by a human being. We want to negotiate important agreements with a person, hearing every quaver in his voice, noting when he crosses his arms, looking into his eyes. To look into someone's eyes – that turns out to be, metaphorically and quite often literally, the key to high-value work in the coming economy."

Colvin stresses that the skills that are going to be needed most in the coming years are not the left-brained skills of business acumen, analysis or management. Instead, they're about "relationship building, teaming, co-creativity, brainstorming, cultural sensitivity and ability to manage diverse employees." Colvin goes on to quote

Oracle group vice president Meg Bear who says, "Empathy is the critical 21st-century skill."

So, empathy is the foundation of all else. "It consists of two elements: understanding the feelings of the other and reacting in an appropriate manner. It's what we crave for – it's what computers will never be able to imitate." Two, it is teamwork. Three, it is storytelling. Why? "Because we are born with an inherent need to tell stories. And because, even when it is not true, we like a good story much better than logic and facts." Four is creativity. "True, computers can be creative. But humans are better at randomness and serendipity. And that's the basis of creativity." And finally, relationships. "No need for further explanation, we suppose," says Colvin.

Beyond Anger and Revenge

On 15 March 2019, 50 people were killed in two consecutive terrorist attacks on mosques in Christchurch in New Zealand. To add to the macabre nature of the killings of people at prayer, the killer live-streamed the first of the two attacks on Facebook Live. Shattering the aura of peace and tranquility in New Zealand, this would go down as one more manifestation of the hateful, divisive and violent politics of nationalism that has been unleashed in the 21st century. It was clearly one of the darkest days in New Zealand's history.

In the hours that followed, the 38-year-old Prime Minister of New Zealand, Jacinda Ardern, called a press conference that set the tone for how she would be addressing this terrible episode. With poise, compassion, empathy and steel, Ardern delivered her message to the killer:

"You may have chosen us. But we utterly reject and condemn you." The 'us' was deeply inclusive, healing the divide that has been violently exploited by other political leaders in recent times. It was also a psychological masterstroke, eradicating the 'out-group' phenomenon by including the Islamic community into the mainstream. By Saturday morning, she was meeting with members of the Muslim community, holding them in her arms as they sobbed. Pictures of Jacinda Ardern dressed in a black headscarf trimmed with gold saying words of condolences travelled across the world, coming as a soothing balm.

In a 19 March article in *The Guardian* newspaper by Eleanor Ainge Roy,[72] the author quoted Paul Buchanan, a security expert for 36th Parallel. According to Buchanan, Ardern's strength is "her empathy" and that "she has excelled in this arena during a time of crisis. She is like the mother of the nation. When it comes to events like this, I think her touch is near perfect" is Buchanan's quote. But empathy needs to be balanced by clarity and even steel when necessary. As Roy writes, "When asked about comments by an Australian senator who sought to blame Muslims for the attack, Ardern called him simply a disgrace."

Later, Ardern spoke in Parliament House and she began her tribute using the Arabic greeting of *As-salaam-alaikum* (Peace be unto you). Six days after the massacre, Ardern went on to announce a ban on military-style semi-automatic weapons, assault rifles and high-capacity magazines. The speed with which she was able to take and pass decisions was unprecedented and an object lesson to other politicians.

Fear and anger are two of the most basic emotions that human beings carry and these are deeply embedded in some of the most primitive neural circuits we carry in our brains.

They are easily activated as they are located in the amygdala and linked to the parts of the brain that are used to govern our senses, muscles and hormones. These circuits comprise a fast-trigger mechanism that enables us to react quickly to the sight or sound of a threat.

Overcoming these emotions requires conscious effort and empathy. Political leaders have for centuries been able to manipulate precisely this primitive mechanism we carry in our brains. Danny Li, a writer for *Slate* magazine, refers to philosopher Martha Nussbaum's new book *The Monarchy of Fear*,[73] in which Nussbaum argues that the emotions of fear and anger are often exploited by politicians and the followers are "radicalized by signs of permission and approval".

Social media has made it even easier to do so as we have the technology that promotes the notion 'that everything worth saying can be said right away'. Retributive anger or revenge is a violent yet unproductive emotion that contains "a burning desire for payback, as if the suffering of someone else could solve the group's or the nation's problems".[74]

Ardern made the choice of empathy and grief over anger and revenge. By refusing to name the attacker, she directed a nation's emotions towards grief and empathy rather than torching them with retributive anger and fear. "He will, when I speak, be nameless. And to others, I implore you, speak the names of those who were lost rather than the name of the man who took them. He may have sought notoriety, but we in New Zealand will give him nothing, not even his name."[75]

Role-modelling grief and empathy

Ardern was speaking at a high school that had lost two students in the attacks. One student asked her, "How are you?" Ardern's reply was gentle and clear. "How am I? Thank you for asking. I am very sad." As Danny Li writes: "Ardern's public emphasis on grief has led New Zealanders to engage in public acts and rituals of consolation and compassion. Across New Zealand, people have been performing the *haka*, a traditional Maori dance, as a sign of respect. Rival motorcycle gangs performed the *haka* outside the Al Noor mosque, the site of most of the killings. The dance was also performed by students at New Zealand's largest Muslim school. This morning, Ardern joined thousands for a nationally broadcasted prayer and two-minute moment of silence in Hagley Park across from the Al Noor Mosque. There she remarked, 'New Zealand mourns with you. We are one.'"

If hatred breeds hatred, empathy breeds more empathy.

Productive Empathy

Paul Bloom, professor of cognitive science and psychology at Yale University writes in his book, *Against Empathy*,[76] that the feeling of pain is all well and good but does not necessarily trigger the right moral response. Bloom is not in favour of lack of empathy; rather he says that just the mirroring of another's anguish is not enough of an act of kindness. It is not empathy that leads one to jump into the sea to save a drowning person or to give money to charity. On the contrary, over-identifying with the other's anguish may lead to a paralysis of action or, if not anything else, just adds to personal distress. Bloom also makes the old point about the doctor who would be unable to do her job if she felt her patient's pain: it is not the doctor's job to empathize with the patient's cancer, but to cut out the tumour.

Our research supports Bloom's assertion that empathy alone does not necessarily lead to action. Emotion is necessary, but insufficient. To be useful, empathic emotion must be directed by reason or by a 'schema' for action, as Vivienne Ming suggests. Otherwise empathy doesn't lead to clear, meaningful action.

Rasmus Hougaard and Jacqueline Carter, authors of *The Mind of the Leader*,[77] resonate with our research when they write: "Empathy is good, but it must be combined with constructive action to have real impact. Empathy without the skill and discipline to stand back, judge objectively and act accordingly is worth little."

That is precisely where a powerful sense of purpose comes in. A doctor must have the empathy to become a reassuring presence for the patient, but it is the doctor's purpose of saving lives or healing people that provides what psychologists call agency, the feeling of empowerment to take action.

Part 3

How Do We Put We Put Purpose Back Into Business?

"Many persons have a wrong idea of what constitutes true happiness. It is not attained through self-gratification but through fidelity to a worthy purpose."

HELEN KELLER

CHAPTER 10

The Future
is Human

"The human condition is such that pain and effort are not just symptoms which can be removed without changing life itself ... for mortals, the easy life of the gods would be a lifeless life."

HANNAH ARENDT

The March of Technology

Nineteen years into the 21st century, we find ourselves at the inflection of a big, disruptive step in technology development, what is being termed as the fourth industrial revolution – the age of massive digitalization, augmented intelligence, robotics and big data.

The first industrial revolution began around 1760, heralding the movement away from human reliance on animals and sheer physical effort to the use of fossil fuels and mechanical power. If the steam engine was the symbol of the first industrial age, electricity and mass production became the symbols of the second industrial revolution that began towards the end of the 19th century. The birth of factories and the idea of 'division of labour' – the first harbinger of what was later to morph into one of the core concepts of management science – emerged in this era. Farm workers were brought in as shop-floor workers and mezzanine floors were introduced to allow supervisors to control the largely unskilled labour, while productivity and efficiency became the defining terms of this era. Chaplin's epic work, *Modern Times*, parodied the descent from a nostalgic age of freedom into an industrial dystopian age.

But, dystopian or not, the industrial age soon became a blueprint not just for organizing factories around productivity and efficiency, but also in shaping how we think about work and leadership. Much of how we organize ourselves even today, especially in our large corporations, owes itself to this era. The church and the military provided the only available models for how to organize large groups of people in organizations. Combined with the fact that knowledge and power was in the hands of the very powerful few, we ended up building the archetypal hierarchical organization. Even today, digital technology may be levelling out the playing field, but such was the strength of the archetypal hierarchical form that it continues to endure to this day.

The sixties saw the birth of the third industrial revolution and the first signs of automation. Electronics, transistor chips and Moore's law, named after Gordon Moore who started Intel, became the heartbeat of this era. Moore was an electrical engineer who examined the data on integrated circuits since their invention around 1959. This was in the year 1965. Moore noted that the number of components that fitted on a chip had doubled every year over the past six years. Moore's prediction was that the trend would continue for another ten years, but in reality the trend continued much after the seventies. The year 1995 saw the birth of the commercial internet and its impact on society was akin to what Gutenberg's movable type had achieved in the year 1440.

But the really big inflection point had to wait until the year 2007 when Moore's law really reached its crescendo, when computing power and storage capacity reached a critical mass and the technology for computing devices to become nodes in an interconnected network became available. A whole new group of organizations emerged that would change the way human beings would live, communicate and work. Music, moving images and news would never be the same again. Software, as the now popular saying goes, began eating the world. Facebook, Twitter, Change.org, the Android platform, Kindle, LED lighting, to name a few, all emerged in the year 2007 and, together, the innovations that came from these technologies dramatically altered the way we live and work.

The Trillion-node Network

For a species that was used to living linearly in terms of navigating the environment, nothing would ever be the same again. The tribal had become global; for the first time in history, the world became part of a gigantic digital network.

We are now entering a new era of cyber-neural systems that are transforming the way both humans and machines operate. Machine learning, robotics and AI are beginning to dismantle every aspect of what we have known about work and about managing our organizations and our societies. A recently published report by industry analyst Forrester details that 10 years from now 16% of all jobs will be automated, resulting in a 7% net loss for human workers. Autonomous vehicles, chatbots and personal assistants are only the nascent forms of a world of artificial intelligence that is emerging around us. Bionic body parts, 3D-printed from inks made of living cells, are no longer science fiction.

The algorithms that can design the materials that can substitute living cells are already here. A computer-enhanced 'generative process' can prototype every kind of product design, as easily as the hundreds of pictures you take on your phone. Block-chains are poised to replace bureaucrats, clerks and back office service agents. AI is making its inroads rapidly.

As Harari writes in his 2018 book *21 Lessons for the 21st Century*,[78] the AI revolution is not just about computers getting faster and smarter. "It is fuelled by breakthroughs in the life sciences and the social sciences as well. The better we understand the biochemical mechanisms that underpin human emotions, desires and choices, the better computers can become in analyzing human behaviour, predicting human decisions ..."

But what about things like human intuition? Can AI ever outperform humans in tasks that demand intuition? The answer is yes. Human intuition, as Harari points out, is nothing but pattern recognition, therefore computers will always be better than us at deciphering patterns. In fact, the synaptic algorithms that we employ in our brains are hardly attuned to the 21st century landscape of complexity. As Yuval Noah Harari writes, "they rely on heuristics, shortcuts and outdated circuits adapted to the African savannah rather than to the urban jungle."

So, if emotions and desires are merely biochemical algorithms that computers can decipher, AI can be better at jobs that 'demand intuitions about other people'. Moreover, AI has two features that human beings simply cannot replicate: connectivity and updateability. No human individual or group can ever match this.

The emergence of the new brain in human beings 70,000 years ago allowed us to develop what David Krakauer, president of the Santa Fe Institute, calls 'cognitive artefacts'.

These typically extend human abilities to reason about the world, amplifying what we are able to do. For example, studying a map provides a spatial awareness that remains in memory even after the map has been put away. In fact, our rapid development as a species had a lot to do with the cognitive artefacts that allowed the human brain to work in ways that far extended its ability to think.

'Competitive cognitive artefacts', a clumsy term, on the other hand, are analogues of what we do, with capabilities that generally surpass our own. So, an algorithm that translates GPS coordinates into a voice that tells you on your smartphone to take a left turn is an example of this. Krakauer's point is that such competitive cognitive artefacts are tremendously helpful, but they provide no spatial awareness. Lose the cell signal and you are lost, as you are completely dependent on the algorithm. But what if the AI is embedded in our bodies? It just becomes an extension of the human brain and the possibilities become limitless.

AI is a competitive cognitive artefact. All deep learning systems layered with neural nets are designed to learn how to learn and Krakauer calls them the ultimate competitive cognitive artefact. And the early signs are obvious: IBM's Watson is far superior at Jeopardy, and Google's AlphaGo is unbeatable at Go. But then these are just games. What is more interesting is how our thinking is going to be shaped by these competing artefacts. "The golden rule of cognition and evolution is use it or lose it," notes Krakauer.

What happens when a rapidly increasing number of competitive cognitive artefacts become all-pervasive in our lives and work? Tiny sensors and micro-processors are building an ever-expanding digital network. As they generate ever-increasing amounts of data, the ability of the network to learn increases exponentially. That is precisely what Mickey McManus, a pioneer in the field of collaborative innovation and human-centred design, refers to as 'the trillion-node network'. By this he means the emergence of a vast and complex network that is creating a reality in which machines can potentially do everything that humans can do. The trillion-dollar question then is, what is going to be the role of humans in such a rapidly accelerating algorithmic world? And, more specifically, what is the role of leadership?

The Future is Human

If you are thinking that we are trying to paint a dystopian picture of the 21st century, the truth is far from it. On the contrary, our position is that the future must be more human than ever before. By this we mean that we will have to consciously and purposefully exercise the very qualities that make us human. From a 21st century context, this means that anything repeatable or routine is out, because there will be an app that can do the same thing cheaper and faster and at scale. Does this mean that we will be able to focus on doing work that is creative and meaningful, rather than mundane and mechanical? More importantly, will it benefit all humankind? These are big questions and there are no immediate answers. For us as authors, that is ultimately what *Rehumanizing Leadership* will be all about: building organizations and societies in which human beings thrive. Also, the 21st century world has become too complex and networked to be understood by 20th century theories of leadership. We desperately need an entirely different worldview based on interdependence.

The Future of Work

Vivienne Ming is not someone you can take lightly. Passionate, evocative and brilliant, Vivienne is a theoretical neuroscientist, entrepreneur and the co-founder of Socos, an independent think tank exploring the future of human potential with machine learning and deep neural networks. Popular for her two talks, 'How to Robot-Proof your Kids' and 'The Tax on Being Different', Ming's interest in purpose comes from a much broader domain, of searching for predictive qualities in individuals. Named one of 10 Women to Watch in Tech in 2013 by the *Inc.* magazine, Ming's research and work is at the sharp cutting edge of how AI and deep neural networks can transform the way we understand human potential. She makes a compelling argument to demonstrate how useful 'Augmented Intelligence' is. At a recent public talk for Singularity University in Johannesburg, she spoke of her Type 1 diabetic son and how she has developed a predictive model of diabetes to better manage his glucose levels. She has also developed the technology to predict manic episodes in bipolar sufferers.

"AI and Machine Learning is profound," as Ming said in her talk. "It will have a profound impact on our society ... and on human potential." Ming goes on to say something deliberately provocative: "Human capital is becoming a toxic asset ... If we don't change the way we build people, they will be vastly less than we think they are." And then, referring to all the professional services in the world including finance and medicine, Ming says that they will be made redundant in the next five to ten years. She adds, "If you know what you are going to advise clients before they ever walk in through the door, I am going to build an AI that is going to do it cheaper, faster and better than you." If routine tasks are going to be taken over by AI, Ming suggests that building more uniquely human skills—in particular, creative and adaptive 'problem exploration' skills—is crucial to building better humans.

You can imagine how keen we were to get Ming's perspective on rehumanizing leadership, especially her views on purpose. Ming began the conversation by referring to 'endogenous motivation', or the self-driven energy that directs behaviour. It is a quality that is closely linked to purpose and is strongly predictive. If people need to focus on ever more complex and creative work, meaning and 'motivational assets' become indispensable. "They are things that are bigger than yourself. All of these things have been studied independently. What was surprising is how much these matter," she added. We asked her what predicted good outcomes at an individual level? "We kept finding again and again constructs like purpose. It's such a strong narrative element. Purpose, though, is hard to define and measure; but people have been studying this empirically, but much less in the business world. What you see is lots in the education space. For example, if you sit students down in class and read them a narrative about a purpose that is bigger than themselves, you see much better performance. In the course, they were talking about real-life cover stories; they were taking well-known individuals and describing their work in terms of purpose, like Steve Jobs or Martin Luther King Jr versus simply giving a chronology of events. It was enough to change the outcomes for the students."

Ming went on to tell us that there are some fuzzy lines between purpose, grit and motivation. "What we found, is that you can construct your own purpose ... for constructing your own purpose, it has to be bigger than you, so your career cannot be your purpose." She spoke about purpose having to be inherently good. Ming referred to another researcher who found evidence that having a positive, pro-social purpose meant something.

We wanted to probe more and ask Ming about her views on the role of purpose in business. We began by asking her about her own purpose. "I see purpose as something that is not fixed, but as a guiding star. It has a longer half-life than other decision-making elements. You go through these little periods where, for five to seven years, you are deeply committed and then you move on, it's your purpose that guides you."

So how would Ming describe her own purpose? "My purpose was to live a life that makes other people's lives better," she begins. "It wasn't narrow enough to drive clear decisions. Now, I say I'm interested in literally building better people. So it narrows, clarifies and expands over time. I talk about neuroscience, economics, machine learning, etc. Seems all over the place, but to me it's crystal clear. I need to understand all these things to serve my purpose. I don't do a lot of abstract macro-economic work, but I use them as tools. So, it's much more crystalline for me. But in other ways it's become more expansive."

Building Better People

As educators, we couldn't think of a better way to state a purpose in which you are out to maximize other people's potential: 'building better people'. For us as authors, we sensed an immediate link between what we have been referring to as rehumanizing and Ming's words. We asked Ming the question: "What is a skill you believe to be future-proof?" Her answer was immediate: "It's not programming or machine learning. In my work and my research,

I find myself repeatedly returning to purpose or, more specifically, the psychological construct of strength of purpose. For a concept that might sound very soft, purpose has very hard, tangible positive returns on life: education attainment, wealth and income, health and wellbeing and even simple happiness. Purpose-driven people likely always have and always will lead richer lives."

We probed further. "Does not strength of purpose take time and commitment to develop?" "Yes", Ming answers, "but there are immediate strategies to cultivate. One of my most valued is to always be ready to walk away if I believe that I'm not serving my purpose. No matter how lucrative the opportunity, how prestigious the job, how profound the potential, my purpose must come first in all of my decisions. I've learned that my life is best when it's not about me.

My life is best when it is not about me. Ten simple words strung together in a sentence that immediately captures the very zeitgeist of purpose and a meaningful life. We are reminded of Emerson's quote: "The purpose of life is not to be happy. It is to be useful, to be honourable, to be compassionate, to have it make some difference that you have lived and lived well." Ming continues, as though picking up exactly what Emerson was thinking of around 150 years ago. "All that defines a purpose is that it's bigger than you and will take more than your life to accomplish. As the saying goes, 'The world gets better when old men plant trees'. You get to build a purpose for yourself. You plant the tree under whose shade you will never rest. Perhaps it sounds exhausting or naïve, but imagine a society of people capable of constructing their own purpose. For what would you sacrifice? That is what will carry you into the future."

Purpose is Defined
by Sacrifice

Why is purpose important from a psychological perspective? "Purpose works for an individual because, in cognitive psychology, it gives you a 'schema' for interacting with the world. So when opportunities arise or when negative things happen, you have a script for dealing with them." This simple secret makes it possible for us to not "treat everything as a *de novo* event". Ming says this forcefully: "It turns out you have a script. It's enormously flattering to be offered Chief Scientist at Amazon." Ming explains what she means: "Whenever I took a job where flattery won me over, it was always negative. I wouldn't have been successful in them, not in the way Jeff Bezos wanted me to. So it's a pre-decision process – a commitment to a set of actions aligned to a bigger goal – so it completely enables agility. This is even more important in a world where agility is becoming more important." Purpose makes for pre-decision and agility. This was a real insight for us as researchers!

Purpose is defined by sacrifice. We wanted to hear Ming explain what that meant. "How fragile can purpose be if it's not real?" she asked. "Purpose means that you must be willing to make a sacrifice. And it should be clear what that sacrifice is. That's what makes it authentic. In other words, there are very tantalizing things you might want to do, but your purpose constrains you. Sacrifice is hard because in the business context, it's hard to live up to."

Our conversation turns to why purpose is not easy. Ming provides four more interesting perspectives:

1. Everyone has to live up to the purpose
Ming talks about the ultimate litmus test for purpose: does everybody really live by it: "... when you define purpose

in generic terms, there's an expectation that everyone is going to live up to the same purpose. If Whole Foods' purpose is to create a sustainable food culture, then everyone has a belief about what the CEO should do about it being acquired. What we see a lot of in the start-up world is incredibly strong wording around purpose, but then the whole thing collapses when the leadership exhibits behaviours counter to the purpose."

It is for that reason that purpose needs to be embedded deeply in the culture, according to Ming "... it needs to be part of the incentive structure of the culture. It has to be lived by the leadership. It can be really hard and culture and leadership is a strangely not-natural process. It's like being a parent. All you want to do is hug your kid and protect them, but you need to know you can't."

2. Authenticity is everything

Ming is convinced that purpose plays a key role in successful organizations. She talks of greater retention, greater performance and lower absenteeism as the three consequences of aligning roles to purpose. The catch for Ming, however, is that senior leaders ought to live by the same rules. "Purpose not lived by the execs can undermine ... the gains ..." Ming goes on to add: "My experience was that there is a repeating instance where companies that had a purpose that they lived and died by were frequently dying by it because their employees were expected to live by it but their leaders were not." She is cynical when she says of many senior leaders, "when you hear them, you don't feel a noble purpose; you just think that they want to feel good about being rich. So it seems as though purpose has to be authentic to work."

3. The War for Talent is Being Fought with Purpose

This is another interesting insight from Ming and she sees this in the context of Silicon Valley; she calls it "part of the ecology of failure in the start-up world." When we ask her to explain what that means, she says: "Everyone in the Bay Area thinks you need a purpose, but one of the standard failure states is a misalignment between the employees and the leadership. If the employees don't see it, then that failure erupts because people get disengaged. If you are competing for top talent – and I'm constantly recruiting against Google, etc. – so a big part of my recruiting is using purpose. But lots of people are selling purpose, and it somewhat devalues our purpose." Ming explains her point: "You can get caught in a systematic process of building a good cover story for what you really want to do, then you have a churn and it's phenomenally difficult to do business in."

4. Inclusiveness Matters, But It's Not That Simple

Ming continues with her theme of the disconnect between what senior leaders do and what they say. "My research shows that if you say, 'Hey, we believe in diversity' and your leadership team is straight, white old guys, this is an action in conflict with your statement." And to drive her point further, she says: "And you would have been better off saying, hey we're here to get rich and to do so with people who make us comfortable." Ming then refers to the research on inclusiveness in the growth of economies and how it is the single biggest predictor of growth. In that context, immigrant and refugees, according to Ming, are positive drivers of growth, but only in inclusive cultures! "But in non-inclusive cultures, it's a drag on the economy," says Ming. "If you're not inclusive, forcing inclusiveness is negative, so I'm suggesting:

if you don't actually have a purpose, forcing one is a drag. It creates an economic drag on the organization."

Ming says that we can end up stacking the organization against itself, by trying to force purpose on to its employees. She explains: "... you have to be purpose driven because you've created a culture that is purpose driven, not because you've said, 'let's be purpose driven'." My personal belief is that it doesn't have to be a noble one. It just requires that you invest yourself deeply, it has to be bigger than you and it has to have a notion of sacrifice. The question is, can you bring a leadership team around it, etc. It's not a marketing strategy and it has to be genuine."

Ming takes us back to the point she made earlier, and she makes it even more forcefully this time: *"Somewhere in there, if there isn't sacrifice or trade-off, then I'm not seeing someone who is serving a purpose. I think of this as a symptom. If I don't see your palms are bleeding, it's hard to see that a purpose is being served."*

CHAPTER 11

Finding Your Purpose

"Let yourself be silently drawn by the strange pull of what you love. It will not lead you astray."

RUMI

Rosanna Ramos-Velita is the Chairman of Caja Rural Los Andes, a microfinance bank that is based in Puno, Peru. Situated at over 5,000m above sea level near the shores of Lake Titicaca, the bank provides micro-deposits and micro-insurance to the country's rural Andean communities. Ramos-Velita has a singular purpose that guides her work: to eradicate poverty. Caja Rural Los Andes is a highly profitable bank that offers an over 30% internal rate of return (IRR). "But we are here to do good," she says. "We try to contribute to solving a serious social problem. Our purpose is to eradicate poverty. Our strategic focus is on Andean entrepreneurs, owners of small family, craft and agricultural businesses."

How does a successful Citibank banker from New York become the Chairman at a microfinance bank in Puno? We met Ramos-Velita in New York to talk about her journey. Peruvian by birth, she has always felt "committed to the betterment of my country". She studied at the University of

Pennsylvania's Wharton School and at the Lauder Institute of International Studies. "That was a time of privilege for me," says Ramos-Velita. "My parents always wanted the best for me. That is how I ended up going to university and graduate school in the US, because it's still the land of opportunity as far as I'm concerned."

From there, she went on to become a senior CFO at Citibank and led business development for emerging markets. The growth of the middle class was the big story, but Ramos-Velita knew that the real opportunity lay in the demographics just under the middle-class level. "I was particularly interested in our consumer finance business, which at that level was all subprime, uncollateralized and very high interest, around 100% APR. What was interesting to me is that it was highly profitable. Here we had relatively poor people taking out small loans, with better repayment than other market segments." Ramos-Velita went to Mexico to investigate more about this phenomenon that fascinated her. There she ended up in a poor village, "really a shanty town where we operated some branches under a different name. The branch manager informed me that most of their clients were women. This was a good thing because they didn't use the loans for consumption; rather, they used it to fund small businesses."

The Awakening of Purpose

What was to happen in this shanty town was to change her life forever. Outside the branch where she was based was a small taco kiosk, a *taquería* run by a woman who was very busy catering to the lunchtime rush. "I struck up a conversation with her and let her know that I worked for the bank just behind her. She stopped what she was doing and came around to give me a big hug. She told me that she got a loan from that bank for $800 and that allowed her to grow her business and provide for her family. Before the loan, she was selling tacos out of a basket. In business terms, we'd say she had a scale problem. With the loan, she worked out in her head that she could repay the loan in a year because she could sell a lot more. She got a second loan and now operates two kiosks, one run by her husband, a former cab driver. "He works for me now," she said with a smile. She also said that with this business, she was able, literally, to put a roof over her head, eat better and she could pay to send her kids to private school.

Ramos-Velita's big 'Aha' moment was that hug. "My investment banking clients never hugged me! I also realized that I could bring all my expertise in banking and capital management to Peru to make a difference in people's lives." She soon left Citibank and, in her words, "put together a business plan, did some serious fundraising and got investors to help me buy an existing microfinance bank in Peru that was underperforming both in terms of profitability and in terms of its impact on society." The hug from her client helped activate her purpose. "Our returns are over 30%. But our purpose is to reduce poverty. This matters because microfinance starts with purpose. We ask 'why?' I've been a banker for over 25 years. I should be able to make money and not mess up. But, I emphasize our purpose all the time – to reduce poverty, to be a financial partner for rural families. And I want to grow."

We asked Ramos-Velita what her shareholders expected. Was it profit or purpose? She replied, "In this space, shareholders want to know more about the people you touch." But it is not the same for the banks in the USA. "Financial services have a long way to go in connecting purpose and profit … the corporate world is still very slow on this front. They are under pressure – or at least they feel that they are – to only focus on the money." When we asked her how purpose affected her employees, her reply was that they needed to be inspired. "With our purpose in mind, they work harder. I see their posts with clients on WhatsApp, I see how committed they are. We call this *compromiso* in Spanish. They all live in Puno, they celebrate with their clients when they have successes in their businesses."

We asked Ramos-Velita to describe how she saw her purpose. "It's because of purpose that we're successful financially. Purpose allowed me to create a successful team. It helped me to believe in myself and believe in my people. Caja Rural Los Andes was there for ten years before I came along with my team. Purpose allowed us to totally re-energize the people, the business and the community."

When she visited the bank the first time, the employees at the bank were not particularly motivated or inspired. "When I got there, I asked about the vision of the bank and I was told that success was defined by one day getting an ATM machine in Lima. That was it! Totally not energizing, or even relevant!" she exclaimed.

The employees told her that she needed to hire consultants to fix the place. "I said, No! We will do it. We are all smart enough and we can do it! What we had was a team that was demotivated and de-energized and we turned that around with purpose. Not only that, but we are turning around families and whole communities."

This story not only demonstrates the motivation that is catalysed through a clear, human-centred purpose, but also how a leader's own personal purpose matters. In the case of Caja Rural Los Andes, the shared purpose had its origin in Ramos-Velita's personal story that came before and after that pivotal moment at the taco kiosk. Shared purpose, then, is closely intertwined with the personal purpose of leaders. However, not everyone who comes from Peru gets to go to Wharton and, through sheer happenstance, gets a great big hug from a client. How else can you go about activating this inner compass?

Crafting your Purpose

Kevin Cox, Chief Human Resources Officer at GE, discussed individual purpose with us. He is passionate about the topic and he started by talking about human courage. "Leaders who focus in on purpose have the opportunity to demonstrate greater courage," said Cox. "They can be a part of something that is bigger than themselves. This has profound benefits for the individuals they lead and organization that they are part of." To illustrate his point further, he spoke about a firefighter's courage: "When they run into a burning building to rescue people, they don't necessarily stop and think about whether such a deed is courageous. They just do this because it is part of the purpose of their job ..."

What he was getting at was that once there is a powerful sense of purpose, one doesn't have to think about it. It almost becomes part of a muscle memory and generates action without the interference of thought process. We wanted to shift the conversation to organizational purpose, but Cox was still focused on individual purpose. He continued to share the following four key questions and explained that at the intersection of these questions is purpose:

1. *What are your personal aspirations?*
2. *What are your passions?*
3. *What are your unique skills and abilities?*
4. *What is most important to you?*

Cox was talking about individual purpose, but there was a clear blueprint emerging here for translating the same into an organization. When we asked him about the challenges of bringing purpose into a shared place, he was quick to respond: "To move people around purpose, you need to drill down to the essence. There needs to be more emphasis on feelings and values, rather than logic and rationale. It is difficult to find a 'rational purpose'. Purpose should transcend the day-to-day. You can't be afraid to emote and think about the underlying passions."

Purpose is Not Rational

"It is difficult to find a rational purpose." Those are important words and serve as an important reminder to us when we start the process of crafting purpose in our organizations. It's not only difficult to find a rational purpose, it is almost impossible. Purpose is actually part of the human brain's reward mechanism; when we experience purpose, we feel 'chemically rewarded', which makes us want to strive more. This goes on to generate a positive spiral that results in more wellbeing. Moreover, these chemicals have biologically protective properties and are good for physical health. People with purpose tend to live longer and have fewer ailments. This just shows how purpose is evolutionarily hardwired into the human brain. It is crucial to the survival instinct.

The problem is finding that purpose. Being emotional in nature rather than rational, it has to first be validated by the deeply unconscious limbic circuits of the brain before it can even be admitted into the more conscious realms of the brain. This means that unless we are able to establish emotional connections with purpose it is totally futile. We will get back to this point when we talk about the relationship between emotion and human motivation, but for now we are going to focus on the crafting of purpose.

Cox shared with us that moving beyond these internally directed questions is an organizational need to put that purpose into an organizational context. He shared with us his own version of the Japanese *Ikigai*[79] framework that he uses to coach leaders on how to merge their own personal sense of purpose with their role. Purpose lies at the centre of four overlapping circles.

Circle 1 (in the twelve-o'clock position): Your purpose must serve an important need in the organization, without which it cannot find expression.

Circle 2 (three o'clock): Your purpose must be something that you care about.

Circle 3 (six o'clock): Your purpose must be something where you have some unique skills.

Circle 4 (nine o'clock): The purpose of the organization fits your own story. In other words, it feels authentic to you, to where you've come from and where you're going.

Small p and Big P

In continuing to delve deeper into individual purpose and the motivation that comes from it, we naturally considered Daniel Pink's groundbreaking 2010 book on motivation, *Drive*. We met with Pink to talk to him a bit more about his findings. Surprisingly, Pink shared with us that the topic of purpose, which along with autonomy and mastery form the basis of intrinsic motivation, needs further exploration. "I think that individual purpose is not one thing, but two things. I only wrote about one thing. The simplest way to explain it is to think of a capital P and a small p," he replied.

For Pink, capital P represents purpose in the way we traditionally think about individual purpose – life purpose. For example it could be something like, "I work for Roche because I want to save lives." This is a powerful performance enhancer, but can be difficult to access every single day. And in the context of many organizations it's a stretch. "For example, if you're working in industrial adhesives, this is harder. I think that capital P is daunting for people. I think the research bears this out as well."

Pink went on to talk about the small p. "The small p purpose is something simpler. It is: Am I simply making a contribution? So if I'm working in a chemical plant my individual purpose might be to help my colleagues get a product out of the door. I'm going to help solve problems. I didn't feed the hungry, I just helped out a teammate."

Pink explained that research shows this to be an important performance enhancer, but we give it short shrift because we're so seduced by the capital P purpose. "I think that it's helpful for people to understand. When I talk about p they heave a sigh of relief because all of a sudden, they feel they can access it."

We talked more on the topic of the small p as this was getting interesting. "I first touched on this idea when I was working on my book *Free Agent Nation*. My methodology was travelling around the US interviewing hundreds of people. I had pages of qualitative interviews. I saw a line repeating itself 'Dan, another reason I left was I wasn't making a contribution'. Not 'making a difference', but 'making a contribution'."

Pink's insight was that the capital P purpose is about making a difference. But the small p purpose is about making a contribution. "I think you need both. I was completely enamoured of capital P. But both are important, and they are not mutually exclusive. To talk about one without the other is actually an impoverished conversation."

Excavating Purpose

We shared with him the insights from our interview with Kevin Cox in which he had referred to "my purpose at this moment in this job". Pink's response was that you have core purpose or life purpose, which animates you as an individual (this is capital P). Then there is the contextual purpose, which expresses itself in this situation at this moment (closer to small p because it should be about contribution). The duality is critical.

We went on to ask Daniel Pink how he had arrived at this concept of small p and capital P. "I think it came from people asking me questions like, 'I work in commercial adhesives and we aren't solving world hunger.' Also, looking at more research, I saw that purpose had a broader dimension than how I thought about it. I'm trying to be a strong believer in simplifying ideas. There is a sense of relief when I mention it. We may not be able to access capital P purpose every day, but we can come up with small p purpose."

Pink explained that a study by Amy Wrzesnieski and Barry Schwartz years earlier had first got him interested in purpose. "They found some fascinating insights. They looked at questionnaires that West Point cadets filled out. They found that the cadets that were most purpose-driven were the most successful. More broad research on pro-social behaviour showed the same thing." Pink went on to tell us about his purpose, "I got to my purpose through trial and error and I came to things. I didn't know I wanted to be a writer until my early thirties. It wasn't early." We asked him to tell us about his capital P. "For me it's about helping people understand their world a little more clearly and live their lives more fruitfully. People have a struggle to slow down and stop to think about how to work a little smarter and live a little better." And the small p purpose? "For me it comes down to learning something new and producing good work. It's more 'me' focused. The fact that I'm learning something new is very important to me personally."

Pink loved the word 'excavated' that we had used in the conversation and he zeroed in on it. "One of the strongest things about the questions you are asking has to do with 'excavating'. A lot of times purpose is something that is discovered and excavated and surfaced rather than something that is crafted, created or confected."

Loving What You Do

Not all of us are either fortunate in knowing what our big purpose is or have done enough excavating to have an idea of what our big P is. For some, purpose arrives early in their lives and it stays with them until the end. Some others find it much later. And then there are some who have been quietly working from their purpose, but have never articulated it in those terms.

Whichever camp you belong to, the one precondition for purpose is that you must love what you do. When work becomes unmoored from passion, it is highly unlikely that it will serve any sense of purpose. As leadership educators, we find it nothing short of tragic when we meet seemingly successful managers and executives who return home every day hollow and bereft of any passion they feel for their work. In one of our leadership workshops, we met a very senior executive who looked like a picture of success in his very neatly cut suit. Then during the late-morning session in which we were discussing passion and purpose, he abruptly left the room looking rather distraught. We caught up with him during the break and he looked like he had had a meltdown. "I hate my work," he confided to us. "I am 47 years old and I have no idea where I am headed." We spent the lunch hour with him privately as he shared his lament. But finally, when we asked him if he was willing to make some big changes in his life, he lowered his eyes and said, "I can't. I've got a big mortgage and I've just bought a new Porsche for my wife."

Steve Jobs' 2005 Stanford commencement address is now legendary for invoking the quest for a calling. "Your work is going to fill a large part of your life and the only way to be truly satisfied is to do what you believe is great work. And the only way to do great work is to love what you do. If you haven't found it yet, keep looking. Don't settle. As with all matters of the heart, you'll know when you find it. And, like any great relationship, it just gets better and better as the years roll on. So keep looking until you find it. Don't settle."

The problem for a lot of people, like the senior executive in the workshop, is that their definition of success is borrowed from what they have assimilated from the outside. Symbols of success like cars, houses and corner suites are seductive, but they turn out to be empty. And by the time they realize that it is empty, it is perceived as being too late. In a 2006 article called 'How to Do What You Love',[80] Paul Graham, founder of Y-Combinator, spells out the difference between making a living and work. "It was not till I was in college that the idea of work finally broke free from the idea of making a living. Then the important question became not how to make money, but what to work on." Working on something rather than chasing prestige that Graham calls 'fossilized inspiration' is about service. Working for prestige and all its trappings is markedly different from what Dan Dennett called the secret of happiness in one of his TED Talks: "Find something more important than you are and dedicate your life to it."[81]

But passion and loving what you do takes discipline. It comes with constraints that are necessary. Graham writes of two constraints that he refers to as the upper bound and the lower bound. The upper bound, 'Do what you love' doesn't mean do what you would like to do most this second; it is about the endurance of working on something with no easy gratification. The lower bound, 'You have to like your work more than any unproductive pleasure' is about not treating work as a chore that is followed by a prize of a mindless pleasure. Rather, what you are working on is itself the prize.

CHAPTER 12

Aligning Organizational and Team Purpose

"Treat people as if they were what they ought to be and you help them become what they are capable of becoming."

GOETHE

In Stephen Hawking's seminal work, *A Brief History of Time*, he shares a retelling of an ancient Hindu myth about the Earth in the cosmos:

"A well-known scientist (some say it was Bertrand Russell) once gave a public lecture on astronomy. He described how the Earth orbits around the sun and how the sun, in turn, orbits around the centre of a vast collection of stars called our galaxy. At the end of the lecture, a little old lady at the back of the room got up and said: 'What you have told us is rubbish. The world is really a flat plate supported on the back of a giant tortoise.' The scientist gave a superior smile before replying, 'What is the tortoise standing on?' 'You're very clever, young man, very clever,' said the old lady. 'But it's turtles all the way down!'"[82]

Aligning and embedding purpose in organizational life can seem like a puzzle of infinite regress, as described in this story; that is, in order to be meaningful purpose must rely on a seemingly endless series of dependencies. However, seeking out these connections is a critical part of creating meaning, since the average human's experience in an organization is exactly that – one of multiple connections and strands of meaning.

In the last chapter, we explored how to align individual and organizational purpose which requires, in our view, the need to create a bridge between the individual's deeper, personal life purpose and the work they currently do in their present context in the organization.

Context is Everything

However, engagement is an ongoing task that has to do with allowing employees to bring their own context to the table. Take the example of ANZ. In their work of embedding purpose throughout their organization, they found that to get teams on board they had to set the stage. And, while they couldn't make it a democratic, bottom-up process, engagement was critical because everyone has different perspectives and experiences. Ant Strong, who leads the strategy team at ANZ, along with Anita Fleming who oversees the purpose project at ANZ, shared with us how they started to build engagement: "The Executive Committee debated every word. Then, we got the CEO's narrative, which left us with the challenge of how to embed purpose more deeply throughout the organization. We thought it was critical to grab people's attention and to get employees engaged."

The strategy team, who organized the process, thought it was critical to grab peoples' attention and to get employees engaged. Their first step was to enroll the top 200 leaders to equip them to answer three questions: why purpose mattered for the bank; how it applied to their business unit; and what resonated for them personally. With that in place, the team then decided to bring the entire employee base together for 56 hours (which allowed for work across time zones) in a single, company-wide conversation via a collaboration platform. This meant that during that time, there was always a conversation happening somewhere around the world, led by their Executive Committee.

The result was that over 15,000 participated and they captured over one million words around the topic of purpose. While this effort built up unprecedented awareness about the bank's purpose efforts, it also revealed the enormous diversity of people's views on the subject, from attitudes about purpose being nothing new to a deep desire to drive values that are more human in the bank's everyday work. In this great experiment, ANZ found that context is everything. In essence, shared meaning means that every individual must find the connection points to her or his own work in order to create their own narrative. "What is clear is that the process of engagement requires top-down direction and bottom-up engagement. We talk a lot about alignment and autonomy. If people bring their own context to the table – autonomy – in the absence of alignment, then we would end up with a myriad of small things being done that ultimately don't shift the needle."

The Rise of the Projects and Teamwork

In addition, work is becoming more and more about teamwork. Antonio Nieto-Rodriguez, author of the new book *The Project Revolution*,[83] shared with us two findings from his research that help us bring teams into focus. The first is the fact that project-based activity is fast becoming the norm in most organizations. In fact, the Project Management Institute (PMI) reports that project work is expected to grow from \$12 trillion to over \$20 trillion over the next decade. They also estimate that approximately 22 million jobs will be created per year through 2027.[84]

These findings corroborate our own anecdotal findings with clients. We have gotten into the habit of asking every group of senior leaders attending a leadership development programme the same question: "Think of your leadership energy as a smartphone battery that gets depleted by leading people, which takes effort. How much of that 'battery' is run down at the end of every day, on average, by leading people over whom you have no direct, formal authority?"

Five years ago, most senior leaders, defined by one to three levels below the C-suite, were giving us responses somewhere in the range between 50% and 60%. Today, we routinely hear upwards of 70%. These are people who run large organizations, oversee multi-million-dollar budgets and have enormous formal authority in their jobs. While this wasn't a formal study, the trend across dozens of leaders each year has been alarmingly clear. What's going on?

More and more, work is not driven by authority but by collaboration and influence. Why? Because more and more critical work is happening through projects and teams, and it is growing fast. PMI reported in a recent survey that from 2016 to 2017, projects that executive leaders classified as 'Strategic Initiatives' grew from an average 38% to 50% of their respective organizations' total projects, representing a 32% increase in only one year.[85]

The second finding Nieto-Rodriguez shared with us is that purpose at the project or team level is increasing rapidly in its criticality. "Organizations are often considering hundreds of different projects. Purpose should be part of the selection formula," according to Nieto-Rodriguez, because "it creates a clear line of sight about how the project aligns to organizational priorities." This is even more critical as projects become strategic. "Organizations often judge projects based on business cases that are always presented in a positive light. They should still be part of the equation, but the purpose of the project engages stakeholders in a much more impactful way," he said.

Similar to helping employees find a relevant connection between a person's life purpose and their job, leaders have an additional task. They must seek to create a connection between the shared work that is becoming more and more the reality of daily life and the organization's purpose. In essence, the gap for most us working in teams looks like this:

The Gap Between Team and Organizational Purpose

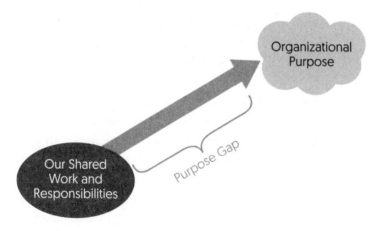

Our day-to-day work in a collaborative team or project-based work environment is clear, but how do we connect that work to the overall purpose of the organization? For example, we might work in a pharmaceutical business whose purpose has to do with helping patients survive life-threatening disease, but if we work in the global IT help desk, what is our connection?

Finding Our Shared Story

This was exactly the challenge faced by one of our clients who was in charge of the global help desk to support employees with their day-to-day IT issues. This is a tough job. When people call for help, they are usually worried, frustrated and angry. Plus, many feel out of control and just want their problem to be fixed. They might be afraid of losing data or hours and hours of work in the face of a hardware or software meltdown. Not surprisingly, this manager had a high turnover of employees because many were simply too burned out by the onslaught of negativity coming from co-workers across the globe.

However, this manager felt their work was important in helping the organization to do its work – helping patients. The IT helpdesk were in 'helping' jobs too, he thought. So he crafted a story for his team based on his very human experience as a father.

"My wife and I have a son who is four years old. He always hated bedtime and we quickly learned why. In fact, he was afraid of the dark and wasn't comfortable going to sleep with the door closed. My wife and I worked out that if we left the door open to his room, some light would come in from the hallway; he would see the light and hear our voices and then he would calm down and go to sleep. We, the members of this team, are the light in the hallway for our fellow coworkers. They are anxious and scared. We're here to help them feel safe and secure so that they can continue on with their life-saving work." He had simply enabled others to discover the asset of meaning, through a simple, humanizing process.

The story worked because it touched every person deeply with the human reality of their shared work. It also created a line of sight to the organization's purpose. It also was memorable. Some employees even put pictures of a dark room with light coming in from a half-opened door in their cubicles and offices as a visual, visceral reminder of their shared purpose.

This story illustrates how this manager closed the gap between the organization's purpose and the team's shared work.

Narrowing the Gap with Team Purpose

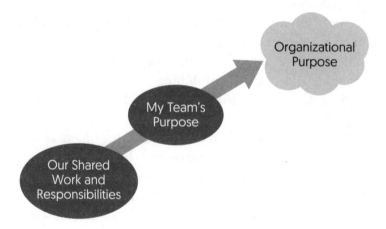

Team Purpose:
It's Personal

Another example of developing a team purpose comes from Steve LaChance of LPL Financial, the largest independent broker-dealer in the US with nearly 17,000 advisors. He is National Sales Manager for a 29-person field-based team of wealth management consultants and shared with us the story of how he came to realize the power of team purpose.

LaChance had been accustomed to working from a sense of deep purpose as a result of serving in the US Navy at the outset of his career. "Defending my country inspired and motivated me," he said. He shared his story at a recent LPL Financial Sales Leadership Conference, where the company's newly crafted purpose narrative was being discussed.

After leaving the military, he joined a publicly-traded financial services company that did not have a clearly stated purpose. Like many other leaders, he found 'growing shareholder equity' unfulfilling.

So, LaChance decided to work on finding his own sense of purpose.

"I realized that we weren't just delivering financial services," he explained. "We were there to help advisors make a difference by enabling them to provide better outcomes for their clients. I could get on board with that."

When LaChance moved to LPL for a similar role, he brought this same purpose with him. Later, when he moved into a leadership role he wanted to understand his team better and to help them achieve their best.

LaChance started engaging his team by leading an off-site session in which he shared his individual purpose journey and how it connected to LPL Financial's purpose as an organization.

"It is key to be transparent," Steve explained. "Once I shared my purpose journey, I asked the team members to send their purpose stories to me."

As part of the process, he anonymously read different individuals' purpose statements with the team at a follow-up meeting. This helped his team to connect to their individual jobs in a deeper and more meaningful way and to arrive at a shared agreement around their team purpose: help our advisors improve outcomes for their clients.

"Connecting the organizational purpose to individual purpose laid the foundation to establishing a common culture," he said.

Recently, LPL Financial helped employees better connect to the firm's purpose by pinpointing it with a simple succinct statement: "We take care of our advisors, so they can take care of their clients."

Guidelines for Establishing Team Purpose

Based on our research and work with clients over the years and building on Steve's story, here are some points to consider on how to go about formulating a team purpose:

1. Don't create the team purpose alone as the leader. Incorporate team members into the process in some fashion. There will be more buy-in and they will see themselves in it. Remember, the goal is *shared* purpose.
2. Team purpose serves as a bridge between the everyday shared work of the team and the overall organizational purpose. It should help team members see how they collectively fit into the bigger picture. This helps bring organizational purpose to life in a very

practical way. It avoids purpose seeming too distant or, worse, a dead concept.

3. Individual, team and organizational purpose may sound like 'purpose overload'. In fact, it is just a process of building a single storyline that helps people see how they fit into the bigger picture.

4. Given the link between individual purpose and team purpose, it is critical that leaders demonstrate a little vulnerability by sharing their respective individual purpose narratives with their teams.

5. Once the team purpose is created, it needs to be reinforced consistently over time.

As teamwork continues to dominate organizational life, taking time out to uncover your team's unique purpose and reinforcing it over time are critical leadership tasks.

"It is incumbent upon project leaders to create a purpose that generates the optimal number of volunteers and the 10% extra discretionary effort that is key to success," said Antonio Nieto-Rodriguez. "The problem is that organizational structures in place are not created to continually address projects. Employees often have a difficult time deciphering how a new project fits within their current operating structure."

In our conversation with Nieto-Rodriguez, we extracted an important point: purpose elevates everything to the human level, beyond task. This creates the energy and alignment necessary to ensure the project work continues as a focus and priority for the organization.

"You need project management skills, but without purpose you can't move into project leadership, which is about inspiration and engagement."

CHAPTER 13

Excavating your Organization's Purpose

"An organization's success has more to do with clarity of shared purpose, common principles and strength of belief in them than to assets, expertise, operating ability or management competence, important as they may be."

DEE HOCK

A paper on building organizational purpose from a well-known consulting firm began with the first step: "Create a clear, well-constructed, aspirational purpose." This was usually followed by the second step: "Now start activating the purpose." Those of you old enough to remember the start of the change management movement will recall similar sounding jargon about defining the future desired state and doing a gap analysis. The problem with this approach is that it is unreservedly mechanical and it assumes that the world is a machine that stays still while we go about our business of either managing change or creating purpose. It also assumes that the process of creating a purpose is different from that of running the business.

There are two important constraints that need to be examined before we can embark on crafting purpose.

One, if creating a purpose were easy we would all be doing it. Secondly, calling purpose 'aspirational' may sound good but it constitutes a dangerous half-truth. Purpose also has to be practical and useful, otherwise it is just an empty marketing slogan. What do some well-known examples of organization purpose look like?

> *"To bring inspiration and innovation to every athlete in the world"* (Nike)
> *"To be disruptive, but make the world a better place"* (Skype)
> *"Helping people be the best in the moments that matter"* (Motorola)
> *"To make people happy"* (Disney)
> *"Doing now what patients need next"* (Roche)
> *"To boldly go where no one has gone before"* (Starship Enterprise)

Notwithstanding the inclusion of the *Star Trek* purpose at the end, these are all real enterprises and they take their purpose seriously. There are plenty more we could add to this list, but for now the question that we want to ask is: how do we really get to the process of crafting our purpose?

Let us go back to what core purpose is all about and reiterate the following aspects of purpose:

1. It states why you exist, what you exist to do or be and your reason for being
2. It clarifies your unique value
3. It states what need you are filling, what is unique to you
4. It states what you are being 'called upon' to do
5. It defines the boundaries of your playing field; what business you choose to be in

6. It can describe whom you serve
7. It can articulate what is unique about your methods
8. It represents that part of your organization's (group's or team's) essence that is always true, regardless of any particular vision of the future

Moreover, the core purpose of any organization must have these essential qualities:

It must be inspiring and energizing
It must be worth your time and energy
It must take a stand
It must be simple, since it reflects what is deeply fundamental
It does not change or is not intended to change (though the meaning might evolve)
It must guide you so that you know what you choose to do and not do
It is not about platitudes

The Problem with Aspirational: Chipotle's Story

One of the attributes often given to purpose is that it has to be aspirational. The problem with aspiration is that it can sound right but be emotionally or operationally inauthentic. Purpose is *the* big question: the reason why we exist and why we feel motivated to do what we do. But purpose can and should also be utilized as a strategic governing mechanism, because it helps align employees and offers clarity on critical decisions – a useful capability in a world where constant change has made strategy seem like the milk in your refrigerator; it is always about to expire.

Until recently, much of the research about purpose revealed the moral and aspirational imperative behind purpose – something about 'making the world a better place' – without uncovering much in the way of warnings. This is concerning – the last thing business needs is for purpose to become another fad or entry into the dictionary of meaningless business jargon.

The story of Chipotle is an interesting case in point here. Ex-Taco Bell Chief Brian Niccol took over as CEO of the beleaguered Chipotle Mexican Grill, Inc., replacing its visionary founder, Steve Ells. At the time of Niccol's appointment to the position of CEO, *The Wall Street Journal*[86] reported that Chipotle had suffered a 40% loss in shareholder value over the past year, amid a series of food safety scares and management's admission that it had neglected essential executional issues critical to success in fast food.

This was a turning point in our research. We had considered Chipotle as an exemplar of using purpose as a way of creating a narrative about something bigger and more humanly important than mere profit. Chipotle famously created a video about *Cultivating a Better World*. Using animation and a soundtrack featuring Willie Nelson singing Cold Play's hauntingly beautiful *The Scientist*, it tells an emotional story of the systemic, environmental and health-related consequences of an overly industrialized food industry. The video sets out a tangible vision for a more humane and healthier farm-to-table world, even for fast food. In fact, it represented an aspirational view of what Chipotle could become and how it could contribute to the world. Just maybe, Chipotle could change fast food itself. Yet there was an obvious disconnect between the food safety scares that led to Chipotle's downturn last year and the communications in this video. Why?

What do our Customers Want?

For perspective, Deborah Wahl, formerly head of US marketing for McDonald's and now the Chief Marketing Officer of General Motors' Cadillac brand, recently told us that purpose works as an accelerator of teams and organizations when placed in a wider business context. At McDonald's, the company purpose for their US business was shaped around 'Honest Food', which was new territory for McDonald's and represented a stretch in a manner similar to Chipotle. This helped transparently answer the public's concerns about ingredient sourcing and healthy eating. "It was motivating – but in a complex business it's not enough to be motivating," she said. "You still have to continuously improve customer service and restaurant operations. You still have to get your digital strategy right. So, we pivoted away from that and readopted the corporate purpose which works much better – 'making delicious, feel-good moments easy for everyone'." In our view, this purpose does a good job of translating McDonald's principles of service, value and convenience into a more aspirational, human experience. Wahl agrees: "Purpose should help you get back to your core, not away from it," she said. "So, when you craft your purpose, you have to start by looking at who you are as a company, who your core customers are, what you really deliver well and what they value. You should never get too detached from that."

What about the need for aspiration, growth and stretch? Wahl agrees this can't be forgotten: "Where a lot of companies get stuck is they stay there and don't take it to the next level. My advice to anyone embarking on a purpose project is to start with the fundamental business drivers. Purpose cannot exist in isolation."

Chipotle's story helped us understand better the role of the customer in crafting a purpose. One of the most important lessons learned about purpose is that it has limits and constraints. Purpose isn't 'blue sky': it has to be firmly rooted in the business model and realistic about its scope. If not, companies run the risk of losing touch with their customers. Perhaps worse, they risk falling into an authenticity trap. But the customer is not the only perspective we have to keep in mind. There is an even bigger constraint, that of the environment we are operating in which provides the context for purpose.

Purpose is Always Within a Context

The task we face is about balancing aspiration with a lucid examination of who your customers are, what they want and what fundamentally drives your business. Yes, purpose should answer the 'big question'. Yes, it should be inspiring. Yes, it should be human and contextual and it should incorporate the idea of service, not just value creation. But having said all that, it must align to the organization's (or brand's) authentic DNA. While Chipotle's purpose embraced an aspiration, it appears also to have been a distraction from the reality of their business. If the purpose is too lofty or distant from the core of your business, it becomes problematic.

This means expanding the 'big question' to questions that look at the 'why' from a variety of angles that force authenticity. Taking examples from our work with clients, we have included the following questions:

- Who are we at our core?
- Who are our customers at their core?
- What is the nature of our relationship with the world around us?

- What is happening in the world that makes us relevant?
- Where can we uniquely and authentically contribute?

In essence, purpose comes down to remembering that the narrative must not just be driving your organization to a compelling, inspiring and motivating future. It must also have a solid foundation that has to do with your past. To paraphrase author Herminia Ibarra's work[87] on leadership authenticity, purpose must paradoxically incorporate the core of who you are but allow your company to stretch its limits. Not an easy task, but that's how you know it's genuinely human.

The Story of Nedbank

Organizational purpose can actually be so aspirational that it is tied to nation building and, at the same time, be tangible enough to drive key decisions. It's not often that we hear this perspective. Yet that is exactly what we gleaned from our conversation with Mfundo Nkuhlu, COO of Nedbank, one of the 'big four' South African banks serving clients throughout the continent.

At first glance, Nedbank's purpose seems solid, but not surprising: 'To use our financial expertise to do good for individuals, families, businesses and society." However, from our research on purpose it is the narrative around the statement that matters. In other words, it is critical how leaders make sense of the purpose in the context and the times in which their organization is operating. Here are four important takeaways we learned from our conversation with Nkuhlu about purpose.

1. Link purpose to your stakeholders

Nkuhlu shared with us that the debate about purpose was the result of Nedbank's Chief Executive, Mike Brown, challenging the bank less than a year ago to look closely at its role in helping government in shaping the future of the country.

"We had always described ourselves as a vision-led, values-driven organization. We realized that the vision is about where we would like to take the enterprise, but it doesn't address why we should be of value to the society. Vision is really internally focused, but purpose is external. It forces you to ask the question from the perspective of clients and society about what's in it for them."

2. Context can be a call to action

Political volatility is a reality in many nations and this has certainly been the case in South Africa. This is the factor that underscores why, as Nkuhlu explained, context creates the perfect opportunity to craft purpose. "When government works effectively, companies can say to themselves, 'We're just going to look at the business side of things because everything else in society is functioning normally.' When it all doesn't seem to work, companies are forced to ask the question of their relevance. If they don't, they could perish." This takes us back to the institutional logic; in order for business to do well, the society in which business operates must do well, therefore business must contribute to the wellbeing of society.

Timing also played a crucial part in getting this conversation elevated to the right level at Nedbank. The pivotal moment was December 2017 at the African National Congress (ANC) leadership conference. "At that time, when Cyril Ramaphosa was elected as leader of the party and, therefore, of the country, a sense of hope came back, but it did not go far enough into confidence," said Nkuhlu. "For example, state-owned enterprises (SOEs) in South Africa appointed new boards and new leadership, but the details around what was going to be done to fix issues like corruption remained unclear."

If the global financial crisis taught us anything, it's that well run, transparent financial institutions matter to a smoothly functioning society and vice versa. Context can be a great motivator.

3. Purpose must correlate to business strengths

Throughout our research, a frequent mistake we kept seeing was the disconnect between the stated purpose and what the organization does best from a business perspective. Nkuhlu addressed precisely this concern: "We realized that we can only bring value to society out of our core strengths and what is germane to our business. We have extensive financial expertise, and this is something unique that we can offer to society. This can come in the form of financial support, but also as advisory services. We had been doing these sorts of things well but, until that time, we hadn't elevated it to the core of our purpose."

The focus on SOEs helped crystallize this meaning-building further. "It was clear from our existing business point of view that we didn't want to just throw money at SOEs; that would be going from bad SOEs to bad banking. But we knew we should provide some measure of support. We are currently clarifying how to do this, guided by our purpose, so that we are not just part of the herd. Currently, we think our financial advisory role will drive us to provide real engagement with the SOEs to ensure that what we deliver is sustainable for them, society and for us," Nkuhlu offered.

4. Make purpose real by linking it to business decisions

Until now, the debate on purpose was a C-suite one. It now started moving out into the conversations and actions of the bank's top 200 leaders. "Even the phrase 'financial expertise' is being debated since there's a concern that it's too generic. We concluded that, yes, any banker must have these skills, but what matters is how we manifest it. What are the proof points?" In fact, Nedbank has already had some success in testing its own understanding of its purpose. For example, Nedbank took over the provision of liquidity of VBS, a bank that had gone under curatorship on the heels of massive fraud. (Curatorship means that its board and executive management are relieved of their duties. A curator is appointed to take over the full management functions of the bank with the purpose of rehabilitating it). In agreement with and underwritten by the South African Reserve Bank (SARB), Nedbank decided to increase the withdrawal cap from R1000 (about US$70) to R100,000 (about US$7,000) per day. For retail depositors, this was hugely positive. Nkuhlu noted that it generated goodwill with about half a million customers who could become solid long-term customers for Nedbank. "Without a purpose, we might have made this a longer process, or we might have done it under regulator duress," he said. "In this case, we asked a simple question: Why are we here and what should we do? When we reported our recommendation to the board, there was full support. The commercial benefit isn't big immediately, but it could be in the long run. This is just one instalment in a series of activities that can help us to clarify our purpose and ensure we are viable for the long run."

More and more in business, and especially in financial services, companies are having to pay attention not just to their economic survival but also to nurturing their role as a positive contributor to society – one that doesn't get paralyzed in the face of complexity.

Looking Inside

The Chipotle story illustrated the role of the customer in crafting a purpose and the story of Nedbank illustrated the importance of the context. We now turn our gaze inwards and look at the two constraints that are internal to your organization. The first of these constraints is your capability, or what your organization can uniquely do. The second is caring, which is about tapping into what energizes your people and building on their empathy.

In our research on purpose so far, we had never heard of anyone who actually had the title of Chief Purpose Officer. That is until we met Lara Bezerra, who was named Chief Purpose Officer of Roche Pharma India in October 2017. Interestingly, Bezerra's previous title was Managing Director and prior to coming to India she was a General Manager with Productos Roche Venezuela SA.

Speaking to Bezerra, we learned that this change in title came about as part of a long organizational purpose journey at Roche India, a wholly owned subsidiary of the Roche Group. There are challenges in taking Roche's well-formulated but potentially abstract global purpose – 'Doing now what patients need next' – and applying it in the context of a large, complex commercial operation like Roche in India. "India is a country of 1.3 billion people and only a tiny fraction of the population can afford or has reimbursed access to cancer treatment," Bezerra said. "This gap between the opportunity to have a real impact on patients and our capability was enormous."

As the company evaluated its opportunities for strategic growth, issues around hierarchical and siloed management processes became evident. "We didn't care about each other's KPIs, only our own," said Bezerra. "We were very command and control. The result was a very reactive, risk-averse organization with no intrinsic motivation. With this set up, agility is limited and you cannot deliver transformational growth, only incremental growth. We needed a new paradigm."

Translating Global Purpose, Locally

Bezerra and her team launched a comprehensive transformational effort. "I asked the organization, 'What is the first thing you'd like me to do?'" The organization was very clear: "we need to create a new shared aspiration". She initially drew on her experiences as a participant in our Duke Corporate Education programme delivered for Roche years earlier. That programme had sparked a conversation among its senior leaders and had resulted in Roche's current purpose. Bezerra knew that while this purpose was powerful, it also needed to be made relevant for the unique challenges of India.

So her team made two crucial clarifications of their purpose narrative. First, in order to have impact on 1.3 billion patients it was clear that 'Doing now what patients need next' could not just be about *some* patients but had to be about *all* patients. Second, purpose could not just be about medicines, but also about the whole health context for patients. This eventually led to the local purpose: 'We inspire people to transform healthcare in India and care for every patient's life through sustainable, innovative solutions'. Through this purpose, they gained clarity about where they could uniquely create positive impact, given their experience and scope: improving the quality and access to healthcare for 1.3 billion people. This would not only require Roche to leverage its existing capabilities but would also necessitate a refocus and a stretch into new territory.

"We knew right away that we would have to inspire government and even competitors to transform the healthcare environment. If we didn't, our innovations wouldn't have any sustainable impact."

What about Strategy?

How does purpose help drive a strategy that delivers transformational results? Bezerra answered: "In places like India or Latin America, you have to have a strategy that's flexible because the markets are so dynamic and complex. We have to be constantly adapting and testing new approaches or else the strategy becomes too rigid. Purpose provides the stable framework for this dynamism to happen." In other words, in order to make choices in a complex, dynamic context you need stable but broad guardrails to anchor all the players.

This is also impacting the operating model. "We realized our intention to be the 'Uber' of healthcare, meaning we must figure out a way to bring together the players in the healthcare ecosystem," Bezerra said. Is this a potential conflict of interest? Roche still needed to care about profits after all, didn't it? "The purpose states that we enhance access to healthcare *and* our products. Otherwise, it would be inauthentic. If I want to increase the market, we have to increase the pie's size. Thus, purpose includes social impact [as well as business impact]. It requires 'both-and' thinking."

All Roads Lead to Leadership

With clarity around purpose, Bezerra and her team addressed important culture changes. Self-organized teams reshaped the company's rewards framework. Traditional pharmaceutical sales metrics were replaced with self-selected 'patient-impact' targets.

It was also important to personalize purpose for employees. "When we ran our purpose workshop, we connected everything to individual purpose," Bezerra said. "We asked how we as a leadership team can be a collective that is driven by higher service and still be able to take care of ourselves and others when we get dragged down by negative emotions like anger and fear." This individualization is such an important aspect of organizational purpose. Without this, purpose can quickly become abstract, lose its value, breed cynicism and undermine transformational efforts.

There are two other noteworthy internally focused leadership dynamics that we gleaned from Roche India's purpose journey. First, the purpose has enabled Bezerra and her team to embrace a holistic, human approach to everything they do. "There have been times when we had to stand up and say, 'We don't know'. We believe in people. This meant we had to be vulnerable to our people and say, 'We need your help'."

Second, Bezerra's role change from Managing Director to Chief Purpose Officer is telling. This was not a demotion – she still leads the entire organization! Here was a general manager who not only thought of herself as a Chief Purpose Officer, but so did her entire organization. This was not a position given to someone in a HR role, but rather to someone who had key managerial oversight of all operations.

Often, titles can be trite. But in this case her new title is incredibly impactful and sends a strong leadership signal. It is a constant reminder that the company not only takes purpose incredibly seriously, but that it is a driver of all business decisions, strategies and operations. The lesson from Roche India is that the inward purpose journey might mean embracing a holistic and transformational approach to your fundamental capabilities and thus your entire business.

Some might think that this human-centred purpose is easy when you're choosing to play in a domain that is already tugging at our empathy strings. We learned that this is not necessarily true. Several years ago, while working at a major pharmaceutical company that is literally saving lives through its oncology drugs, we were surprised at how little executives spoke about patients. In one strategy debate, 'science' was routinely mentioned more than 'patients'. One senior microbiologist-researcher even admitted to me that "in 13 years at this company, I've still not met a real patient." This caused us to question the obviousness of purpose in businesses that deal in life and death.

It is for this reason that we learned that you cannot take employee motivation for granted. It leads us to the second internal constraint – caring. This is about explicitly tapping into what energizes and motivates your people from a human-centred, empathetic perspective, nurturing it and deepening it.

How Human-centred Purpose can Create New Value Streams

We were fortunate enough to meet with George Kellar, Executive Director of the Zen Hospice Project in San Francisco. A former software engineer and executive at a major tech company, Kellar showed us around the beautiful Victorian mansion located in a quiet neighbourhood where the residents (not 'patients') live out their remaining days.

According to Kellar, there are over 43 million unpaid caregivers in the US who struggle with a healthcare system designed around curing, not caring. Zen Hospice Project is trying to disrupt that premise. "Our purpose is to serve the terminally ill and to help them live fully until the end of life by offering them comfort and care, and also to serve their caregivers by helping them build resilience and self-care skills and habits," he said.

The Zen Hospice Project provides a great example for business leaders on how purpose flows from caring – literally. Kellar explained: "By placing the resident – the human being – in the centre of the system, we developed much greater compassion for our residents and what they are going through. This awareness freed us up to reimagine the entire experience from a new lens that includes their support network." As caregivers themselves, everyone at Zen Hospice is deeply motivated by a singular focus on caring for patients and the system of care that surrounds them. By allowing them to reimagine the experience of death, they were able to create together something that had an enormously positive impact on the lives of families going through this painful experience.

This clarity of the caregiver's role is enabled by core beliefs and principles that guide the human-centred purpose. "We base our approach on three principles that emanate from Zen Buddhism: self-awareness, or being present; non-judgment; and acknowledgment of suffering," said Kellar.

These provide clear guidance on behaviours, adding pixels to the otherwise fuzzy picture that a simple purpose statement might deliver. The focus on the residents' experience also caused a complete rethink on the setting. Instead of a clinical, sterile environment, residents live in a house with a home-like aesthetic. Each resident has a totally customized meal plan. A beautiful garden is located in the back to sit, meditate, or just enjoy the flowers. The smell of baking cookies wafts from the homey kitchen.

The clarity of purpose also guides several important operational procedures, which are not necessarily for everyone. For example, the Zen Hospice Project's Guest House facility's focus on preparing residents and families for death means that visitors are encouraged to leave by 9pm so they can care for themselves and build the resilience necessary to cope with the challenging circumstances. Not all families resonate with this way of providing end-of-life care. Employees, however, see these guidelines as essential to delivering holistic care to the family system.

In this way, Zen Hospice showed us how critical it is to nurture and guide the underlying motivations of employees to be of service. Not only does it sustain shared focus and energy in the face of difficult circumstances, but this inward focus also helps unlock a creative approach to providing human-centred experiences based on deep empathy.

Zen Hospice Project's purpose has also enabled them to invent new business models. Because of their focus on caregiving, they now offer educational programmes to bring their holistic caring approach to the caregivers and other large healthcare providers around the country. "Our focus on a human-centred approach to caring for the terminally ill that embraces support and family, makes us uniquely positioned to teach emotional skills to all caregivers – whether professional, family or volunteer caregivers," said Kellar. "So, we imagined a way to meet this need and provide it to people beyond our four walls."

This purpose-led expansion of its business model has been pivotal. While Zen Hospice closed its residential caregiving facility in 2018 due to financial constraints, its clarity of purpose combined with its deep, practice-based experience with end-of-life care enabled it to reposition itself purely as an education provider through its Mindful Caregiver Education and Volunteer Caregiver programmes. And, as Kellar suggests, this pivot actually increases their impact in the caregiving community. For Zen Hospice, purpose has provided the ultimate anchor in value delivery.

Human-centred Purpose is Imperative for All Businesses

We would argue that nurturing a human-centred approach focused on service is equally imperative in businesses that are not life-critical. For example, the email marketing company MailChimp has managed to completely reinvent how small businesses can communicate with their stakeholders. MailChimp's Chief Marketing Officer, Tom Klein, explained to us that their purpose is 'to democratize technology to empower the underdog'. MailChimp's empathetic approach to small-business owners put them, as Klein says, "in their corner". In fact, Klein spoke about how many of their employees identified deeply with their customers, having been small-business owners themselves. This helped them reframe their 'freemium' offerings. Instead of using free email and marketing automation as a means to get customers to pay, their purpose helped them to ask: "How do we make our customers happy or even delighted to pay because they're growing so fast? The freemium offering is about getting people to learn, not just a restriction on volume. We only grow when our customers grow."

Lessons Learned

The good news from both the Zen Hospice Project and MailChimp is that by tapping into basic human empathy and the fundamental human motivation to care for others, we can more easily reimagine human experiences in a way that delivers greater value, however defined. Some lessons from both companies:

- Put the 'customer' at the centre of your purpose, not your product or company. Those figure in later, so don't start there
- To do this, ask: 'Whom are we serving and why?' At its core, purpose is about service to others, just in a business context
- See your customer in context. By building empathy, you're more likely to see other opportunities to serve the customer and, maybe, even other stakeholders
- Look for hard trade-offs. If your purpose isn't forcing tough choices, it's not clear enough

If we stick to what is radically human, meaningful innovation is within reach.

CHAPTER 14

Using the Purpose Framework

"Your system is perfectly designed to give you the results you're getting."

W.E. DEMING

We were in conversation a year ago with the CEO and his team of a manufacturing organization that we don't wish to name for obvious reasons. We asked him about the purpose of the company and he turned to his head of Human Resources who read out their purpose statement. It had the words 'excellence through growth' and 'world-class'. We were impressed by the loftiness of the statement and asked them how they had developed it. "Oh, it was hard work!" the CEO said, followed by much laughter from his team, eager to affiliate with the CEO's humour. "We went for an off-site and we took along a facilitator who worked with us, and there it is!" added the Head of Human Resources. We must have looked a bit puzzled and so she added, "We made sure we then communicated with the next level and asked them to cascade it downwards. It is now on our shareware and all our internal communications."

We don't want to labour the point any more. Needless to say, a year later when we were back in the same organization and asked the CEO how the purpose work was getting along, he said, "It's a journey and we are on it. Right now, we need to focus on getting our strategy set for this year, but we will make sure that we keep on track with our purpose." We have seen other variations on the same theme. In some organizations, we have seen genuine intent on the part of the executive team to involve the whole organization into the process of developing their purpose. But again, a few years later, it is forgotten because it just did not stick. To the point made by Denise Pickett at American Express, purpose must be institutionalized. When great companies demonstrate that purpose works, they are approaching it from a very different perspective.

To go back to Rosabeth Kanter's work on the two types of logic – economic logic and institutional logic – great companies are able to operate effectively on both logical fronts. While economic logic provides the permission for your organization to exist, institutional logic gives it the energy and the reason to exist. One without the other is incomplete. "You have to know where your energy comes from," says Alan Jope, the new CEO at Unilever. "Responsible business can be profitable!" he adds. "A sense of purpose infuses meaning into an organization, institutionalizing the company as a fixture in society and providing continuity between the past and the future," wrote Kanter in her November 2011 HBR article "How Great Companies Think Differently".[88]

Four Perspectives

In our experience of working with several great companies with purpose, their leaders get the institutional and economic logic right by developing four clear perspectives.

1. Context: the environment we are operating in
2. Customer: the recipient of our service and/or products
3. Capabilities: what we are capable of providing
4. Caring: what we stand for

The first two perspectives come from being externally focused through figuring out what is happening in the environment they operate in and with the customers and stakeholders they serve. The second two perspectives are internally focused and are in close touch with the 'inside' of the organization, its people and its capabilities. We are consciously using the term perspectives here, as it takes effort to make sure that the work of knowing what is happening externally and internally is the work of leadership. The two perspectives inform and shape not only the strategy of the organization but also the processes, systems, tools, products and the services of your organization.

External Perspective:
Context and Customer

Walter Isaacson's biography of Steve Jobs reveals all the shades that the genius possessed. There is one revelation from his work that is pointedly relevant to our discussion. Isaacson writes about Jobs' Wednesday morning meetings, which were left unstructured and without an agenda. Power-Point slides were strictly off the table and the meetings began with the question, 'What's next?' As a result, Apple never lost perspective with what was happening in the environment and was always able to stay ahead of the others.

Steve Jobs saw an opportunity where Sony saw a threat. His reading on how digital technology was converging diverse industries allowed him not only to build the iPod, but also to change the way we would listen to music forever. His famous quip, "People don't know what they want until you show it to them. That's why I never rely on market research. Our task is to read things that are not yet on the page." Jobs was a master at the external perspective and was able to pick up weak signals faster than most others. 'What's next?' is not a question you ask at the occasional off-site, but is a strategic question that guides us to being in close contact with the context in which we operate.

There is another hard edge to this, which is not obvious. Unless you make the time for this work it is easily ignored. Leaders must free up time for unstructured work: customer visits, regular 'what's next' meetings, building external networks and participating in external activities are not something you do outside of your regular work, this is your regular work!

The external perspective has received a boost in recent times thanks to the field of design thinking. The most well-known example is of Doug Dietz, an Innovation Architect at GE Healthcare. Dietz has an inspiring TED Talk in which he recalls the journey to designing an MRI scanner for paediatric patients. In his talk, he narrates the time when he saw a little girl who was crying on her way to a scanner that was designed by him.

That was a transformative moment for Dietz as he suddenly saw the situation from the perspective of the little girl. "The room itself is kind of dark and has those flickering fluorescent lights,"[89] he remembers in his TED Talk.

And then he says, "That machine that I had designed basically looked like a brick with a hole in it."

Traditional MRI machines are practically of no use when it comes to children as most children are frightened of them and are also not able to stay still inside. The solution has been to use straps to keep them still and to sedate the children. This is traumatic not just for the children but for the parents too.

Tom and David Kelley, in their book *Creative Confidence*, provide an account of Doug Dietz attending Stanford's design school for a workshop. That workshop gave him the perspective he needed. Rather than focusing on the technology of the scanning machines he was designing, he learned to see the product through the perspective of the customer, in this case the little children.

It began by Dietz spending time observing and gaining empathy for young children at a day care centre. He spent time trying to understand what the children went through by spending time with child life specialists. He sought help from experts at a local children's museum and doctors and staff from a couple of hospitals. He also asked for help internally in GE and got together a small volunteer team. And then he went on to build the first prototype of what would become known as the 'Adventure Series' which was installed as a pilot programme in the children's hospital at the University of Pittsburgh Medical Centre.

These scanners have proven remarkably successful in reducing children's anxiety and thus reducing dramatically the need for sedation. How? Scanners are transformed into make-believe stories through an ingenious use of decals and designs. Each comes with a story, about a pirate or a dragon in a castle for example. The child is not only in the story, but is also the hero. In this way, Dietz has transformed a cold, mechanical and frightening process into a fun, engaging journey for a sick child.

So the key questions in the external perspective are:

Context: *What is the environment that we are oper-
            ating in?*
            What is changing?
            *What is happening at the edges of our
            industry/field?*

Customer: *What do the people we serve need and want
          in their experience of life?*

The external perspective enables you to look at your organization from the outside-in. It may sound trite on paper, but it is genuinely difficult to do. 'When was the last time you met your customers?' is a question we often ask our senior clients, and it is often met with an embarrassing silence and the shuffling of feet. 'What's happening in the world that is currently occupying your thoughts?' is another question we ask. We ask them if they are reading enough; we ask them to comment on the geopolitical changes in the world. Great leaders are able to draw the world in through large windows that they keep deliberately open.

Internal Perspective: Capabilities and Caring

Think of the external and internal perspectives as two different rhythms with two different energies, one going outward and one turning inward. The internal perspective is about an awareness of two critical factors: what are our capabilities and what energizes our people.

We once ran a large-scale leadership programme with a sizeable insurance company. The engagement scores were not looking great and morale was faltering. Part of the programme we were running was trying to address these very issues. When we walked around inside the offices, we noticed a distinct lack of energy in the conversations that people were having. From interviews with the underwriters and the people in the offices, we realized that most of them had never met a customer. We went on to organize a half-day event in the office and brought in four customers. One of the customers was a woman called Sally who told a story of how, 15 years ago, she received a call from her husband's office informing her that her husband had died of a heart attack. She spoke of her whole world collapsing around her. She had two young children and no idea what to do.

Her sister came over to stay and, after a couple of days, asked Sally if she knew if her husband had insurance. They managed to find the papers somewhere and with trembling hands Sally made a phone call. Sally talked of the person at the other end of phone who, with great care and empathy, took Sally through what she was entitled to. According to Sally, the person went out of her way to comfort her. Sally ended her story by saying, "Thank you, whoever you were. Thanks to you, I was able to put my kids through college." There was not one dry eye left in the room. Suddenly there was a palpable sense of purpose in what just some minutes ago was a bland office, devoid of energy or emotion.

The late Sumantra Ghoshal used to refer to this internal perspective as 'the smell of the place', the stuff that either gets your people energized or otherwise. Slightly away from the old centre of Cambridge, just off Madingley Road leading to the Institute of Astronomy, is Churchill College, home to 32 Nobel Laureates, mainly in science and technology.

On the campus of Churchill College, on the other side of the big green playing fields stands the striking looking Møller Institute. When you visit the Møller Institute you instantly get what Ghoshal was referring to. Every single person who works there, from the gardener and the chef to every member of the staff simply radiates the energy of caring for their customers. Time and again, on every survey that is filled out by participants on Møller programmes the feedback always refers to the quality of service provided by the staff.

Gillian Secrett is the CEO of the Møller Institute and Fellow at Churchill College. Her own purpose is to develop leaders to maximize their impact to benefit the organizations in which they work as well as society as a whole. Radiating presence and gentleness, she inspires everyone at the Møller Institute to bring out the best in themselves. A genuine passion to be of service and to creating a caring learning environment is what the Institute provides. Gillian knows its capabilities and makes sure that it never falters. "The ultimate test of practical leadership is the realization of intended, real change that meets people's enduring needs," said James MacGregor Burns, the doyen of Transformational Leadership. It is fitting that the library at the Møller Institute is named after Burns.

When our people feel that their work is contributing towards meeting 'people's enduring needs', they start caring about what they do. They are energized and they are more likely to bring out their best selves. The questions that we as leaders have to ask are:

What are the conditions under which our people can thrive?
What stops our people from bringing out their best selves more often?

*How do we engage with the purpose that our people carry
with them as individuals?*
*How do we help them connect their purpose to that of
the organization?*

The other internal perspective is about our capabilities. It seems easy enough for leaders to know what the capabilities of their organization are, surely that is what runs your organization! But it is not that easy. "To know that we know what we know, and to know that we do not know what we do not know, that is true knowledge," said Copernicus. But capabilities are not just about knowing what we know and what we do not, it is more about the knowledge of what we uniquely provide the world. As a result, it is also about becoming critically aware of our relevance.

When Lara Bezzera took over as the Country Head of India for Roche, she realized that she had to clarify the purpose for their entire business in India. At a strategy workshop with the leadership team, Lara asked the team what Roche would need to change as a whole if it were to deliver according to plan in the year 2030. Another question that the team grappled with was, 'If Roche sells this company in India and we bought it, what would we do?'

Bezzera told us about what Roche India's culture would need to be like if it was going to activate what it innately cared about delivering. So they came up with the following culture principles:

- *Bottom-up, self-organizing, emergent*
- *Flexible, responsive, on the edge*
- *Like a jazz jam session*
- *Vision-centred, value driven*

- *Holistic*
- *Playful – can fail*
- *Deeply green – concern about social impact and human; Sustainability thinking; Systems thinking*
- *Thrive on diversity (embrace 'both-and' thinking).*

It was not going to be easy. "There were times when we had to stand on the stage and say, 'we don't know'. We believe in people, but we had to be vulnerable to our people and say we need your help."

So, the key questions in the internal perspective are:

Capability: *What do we uniquely provide the world?*
What can we uniquely do?
What do we need to get great at?

Caring: *What ultimately do our people care most about when they are motivated and energized?*

The Framework

The purpose framework is formed out of four perspectives, two internal and two external. These perspectives are actually constraints that are necessary for crafting a purpose that is at once inspiring and pragmatic. The external axis spanning Context and Customer provides the outside-in constraints on purpose. The internal axis spanning Capabilities and Caring provides the inside-out constraints on purpose. The four constraints of Context, Customer, Capabilities and Caring together build a dynamic framework in which choices and trade-offs need to be made. Now it starts getting interesting.

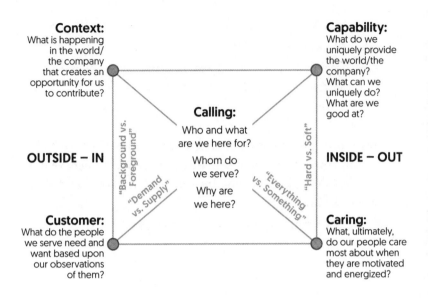

Axis 1: Context and Caring

Making the choice to focus on what we really care about and how that is relevant to what is emerging in the environment

Axis 2: Customer and Capability

Narrowing the space between what customers need/want and what we are great at. What do we need to get better at?

Axis 3: Context and Capability

Making the choice between what is happening outside and what we are uniquely able to provide

Axis 4: Customer and Caring

Making the choice between what customers need/want and what brings out the best in our people

As we begin to have these conversations right across the organization, we slowly begin uncovering what our purpose is at the centre of the four axes. It culminates with the core question: 'Why are we here?' Purpose is oblique in that it emerges when we start taking away what it is not. A quote attributed to Michelangelo when asked how he had managed to sculpt something as beautiful and exquisite as the statue of David was that David was always in the marble and all that he had to do was to take away the bits that were not David.

The Process of Crafting Purpose: Four Stages

'Our purpose is to shape a world where people and communities thrive. That is why we strive to create a balanced, sustainable economy in which everyone can take part and build a better life.' This is the purpose of ANZ Bank and it was meticulously crafted through the following four stages:

Stage 1: Excavation

The excavation stage is where the journey to purpose starts. It begins with leaders reaching deep into the very soul of the organization in its values and its story. The seeds of organizational purpose are to be found either in the story of a founder or founders or in the very beginnings of the organization. We are not saying that the past represents the purpose of the organization; the past simply carries the story of why this organization came to exist. 'To put a dent in the universe' stayed as Apple's purpose in one form or another, and it was clearly a product of the genius and gumption of Jobs. The excavation stage is also important for allowing the identity of the organization to emerge.

'How did we begin?' is a rich and evocative place to start in the exploration of purpose.

This process can also be emotional. For ANZ, a thorough examination of its 180-odd-year past came to an emotional climax the morning after an evening reception held for its top leaders in the ANZ Banking Museum, located in a beautiful, Victorian-Gothic building in downtown Melbourne. One leader offered that he had been unaware after all his years working for ANZ that ANZ was older than Melbourne itself! It had started on the shores of Port Phillip Bay financing the wool trade with Britain in the late 18th century. His insight was that despite ANZ's growth by acquisition over the years it had remained, "a community-centred bank, focused on helping people to thrive ..."

Stage 2: Deep Inquiry

'Why do we exist?' becomes the key question here, pushing us to conduct a rigorous examination of our place in the world. Ultimately, it is not the products and services you sell that defines why your organization exists, but the enduring societal need that you are serving. Louis Kahn, the great American architect, used to ask, "What does a house want to be?" For Kahn, the purpose of architecture was 'the thoughtful making of space'. The stage of deep inquiry helps us to examine our beliefs about the world and is a critical stage to gauge relevance. The second stage of deep inquiry is done using the four constraints that we spelled out earlier.

At the end of the stage of deep inquiry, a semi-formed proto-purpose starts emerging at the centre of the framework. Now is the time to test the proto-purpose.

Stage 3: Socialization and testing

Now is the time to engage with as many individuals and groups in the organization. Test the 'proto-purpose', let people play with it and engage with it. It is remarkable what happens when you share an idea with a diverse group of people who want to contribute. What unfolds is a rich tapestry of many hues and colours, each adding to the original. ANZ engaged in a deep and broad process; however, what matters from our research is that you find as many angles and perspective on these core questions as possible.

Stage 4: Institutionalizing

This step is not just about embedding purpose in the hearts and minds of people. It is also about making it part of the DNA of the organization, including strategy, operations and policy so that it is a living, breathing purpose. Ant Strong and Anita Fleming at ANZ shared with us that key to institutionalizing the bank's purpose was allowing the Strategy Team to lead it. "Situating it in the Strategy Team really helped. It made it about the business. It makes it clear that it's linked to the core of the business and it also gave us access to the CEO," they stated. Other aspects to ANZ's institutionalization process involved integrating purpose with other foundations of the business, such as brand, values, leadership behaviours, CSR, business decision-making frameworks and governance. Tom Klein, MailChimp's Chief Marketing Officer, suggests that institutionalization means allowing purpose to do its work in framing strategy: "If we find something that fits with our purpose, we must incorporate it into our strategy. Without purpose to perform that role, your strategy can become a bit static."

In addition, we've uncovered numerous examples – at ANZ and Nedbank in particular – where 'proof points' are cited as key to making purpose real. At Nedbank, critical decisions on how it managed a bank under curatorship were directly linked to purpose. At ANZ, key decisions about what kind of companies the bank would take on and which it would exit drove home the hard boundaries of purpose. Since ANZ's purpose is about shaping a world where people and communities thrive, the bank decided to exit specific industries that they believe are not supporting healthy, thriving communities in Australia. Saying no to potential business is one of the surest, most concrete signals that purpose is in your organization's DNA.

Finally, institutionalization means looking beyond just operations. It is very much about building a systemic, networked view of the company and its place in the world. A critical factor in MailChimp's institutionalization of its purpose, democratizing technology to enable the underdog, is its ongoing attention and support of small business owners. Tom Klein shared with us that MailChimp had completed a project helping small-business owners in Alpharetta, Georgia, a suburb of Atlanta (MailChimp's headquarters), to perform better during the holidays: "These are folks who take risks but add so much to the local community. What they all have in common is that they don't have a lot of technology mastery. Many of us have run small businesses so we have a lot of empathy for these customers."

The Purpose-driven Leader

A key insight from our work has been that purpose exists at all levels. Much of the conversation about purpose so far has been at a strategic level, among thought leaders in Davos or the boardroom. The discussion has rarely joined up with two other critical areas where purpose exists: the individual employee's sense of personal purpose in their work and the team's purpose.

For individuals, it's vital that we build organizations where we can all realize our 'small p' purpose, as Daniel Pink calls it, which is about how we contribute every day – in contrast, or in addition to, the 'big P' life purpose that has become fashionable. Even if our current job is not quite our dream job, we still need to feel we are making a useful contribution through our work. This individual sense of purpose has to fit with the broader corporate purpose. We call this the purpose 'line of sight'.

Our research suggests many organizations still struggle to create that line of sight. Take the pharmaceutical sector to pick one. There could hardly be a sector with richer potential for inspiring purpose than one which produces products that actually save lives. In a given company, senior leaders might feel confident that they have a clear, customer-focused, inspiring and relevant purpose. Product managers and laboratory-based scientific staff will certainly be able to see a direct link between that purpose and their work. But what of an employee in accounts payable? Do they feel ownership of the purpose and play a part in its success? How about the IT services manager or the fleet manager? In large companies, hundreds or thousands of employees fall into these categories. They might appear to be a step removed from the purpose – yet their contribution is vital to the successful functioning of the company.

Leaders cannot neglect this group. Nor can they take for granted that those whose work more obviously aligns to corporate purpose have internalized their line of sight. Rather, they need a three-pronged approach. First, they must go the extra mile to translate corporate purpose for their people authentically, using their own narrative.

Secondly, they have to recognize their unique role as a leader is to nurture the small p purpose of every employee. A sense of drive to make sure that customer accounts are in order or that the enterprise IT systems are quick, reliable and secure are enormously valuable to the company – and should not be ignored in the effort to establish a corporate purpose.

Third, leaders must internalize the responsibility they bear to foster a sense of team purpose. This means cultivating a sense of why specific teams exist and their role in the functioning of the organization.

A Continual Task at all Levels

Creating purpose is an ongoing task for leaders at all levels. Companies which have an effective purpose recognize that it is not a one-off event where purpose is defined, added to the corporate brochure, put up on the wall and then just allowed to sink beneath the waves of corporate memory. Purpose has to be a living, breathing idea. That demands the engagement of leaders at all levels of a business at every phase in a purpose journey in shaping purpose when needed and in keeping it relevant for those that have it. To summarize, we propose that purpose-driven leaders embrace three critical tasks:

1. **Translate and narrate purpose.** Leaders have to continually join the dots between the corporate purpose and business decisions. A decision that looks obvious in the management team meeting is not obvious for someone outside the room, let alone an employee in another office or another territory. How does a new product, a new hire or even a challenging redundancy announcement relate to purpose? Effective purposeful leaders continually refer back to purpose in their internal and external communications alike, and they make sure to communicate continuously. There is an old Native American saying that important news needs to be said three times: once for each ear and once for the heart.[90] That certainly applies to purpose in business.

2. **Start conversations about team purpose.** One of the perks of leadership in business – and one of its responsibilities – is the power to start conversations. Leaders in the middle of organizations cannot rewrite a corporate purpose, but they do have the power to talk

with their team members about how the team contributes to the corporate purpose. Do you have a clear, one-sentence definition of your team's purpose? Would your team members say the same thing? If unsure, ask them individually to test their views, then hold discussions to shape a shared view. Once established, refer to it continually to keep it alive and relevant.

3. **Help unlock 'small p' purpose.** Helping employees to understand and fulfil their personal purpose is hugely powerful. We know from multiple studies that intrinsic motivation trumps extrinsic – that is, incentives and rewards – when it comes to improving performance, especially for high-value creative work rather than repetitive or mechanistic tasks. A sense of personal purpose is aligned with employee engagement and satisfaction. It connects personal motivation to the organization's purpose. Use coaching techniques to help individuals identify their personal purpose and shape personal performance indicators to align with that purpose, as well as the overall business and team objectives.

It may have come to prominence in the wake of the last financial crash, but purpose is here to stay. It provides a stable point of reference for leaders in today's volatile, uncertain, complex world. As the world shifts around us, knowing what we stand for is priceless: with shared purpose, we can build businesses that are truly agile and can operate at pace, freed from 20th century models of management control that are based on the factories of an earlier industrial revolution. Rehumanizing leadership and remembering that we are purposeful beings is at the heart of business success.

Epilogue

"We shall not cease from exploration, and the end of all our exploring will be to arrive where we started and know the place for the first time."

T.S. ELIOT

Ever since the dawn of civilization, human beings have been driven by a need to question and explore. "The important thing is not to stop questioning. Curiosity has its own reason for existing," said Albert Einstein in one of his many noteworthy quotes. The early explorers charted new geographical landscapes that spanned oceans and mountains, relying on maps and sextants, compasses and the promise of discovery. Fusing a sense of adventure with an innate human curiosity for looking far over the horizon, they braved the natural elements to discover new worlds. The odyssey of the human mind found expression in the Homeric epics as well as in science and art. "I dream of things that never were, and ask, 'Why not?'"[91] was Bernard Shaw's way of describing the art of the possible and the restlessness of the human mind that seeks answers.

To ask 'why?' and 'why not?' we must leave behind the comfort of knowing, for comfort can bring complacency in its wake. Siddhartha slipped out of the palace gates one night, turning his back on all the riches and luxuries of being a prince and walked into the forest where he wandered for six long years. He simply had to leave because he could not bear the thought of a life of comfort, having come face to face with the eventual reality of illness, suffering and death that spares no one. Siddhartha turned his back on not just the comforts of his palace but the comforts of his mind to find the roots of human suffering, a journey that transformed Siddhartha the prince into the Buddha. Leaving the comforts of one's home is the first necessary step in the journey of the hero. The home is not just the place one belongs to, it is a place of comfort, of worldviews that are familiar and a world that we have learned to accept as being right.

The hero leaving her home in search of new lands and coping with the challenges that come in the way, is a much-loved metaphor in all societies and cultures, not just for the discoveries of new lands but also the discovery of who we are. Joseph Campbell, author of *The Hero with a Thousand Faces*, poignantly summed up this most archetypal myth of all when he said: "We must be willing to get rid of the life we've planned, so as to have the life that is waiting for us,"[92] evoking the excitement of self-discovery.

We have come a long way since the days of the early explorers. The 21st century explorer's journey is one that spans the complexities and nuances of an interconnected, digital world in which the looming promise of artificial intelligence is being offset by the problem of leading in a post-truth world. The gap between technology and human ability to use the same technology for creating a better world has never been greater. So is the gap between a networked, interconnected world and the growing forces of nationalism and protectionism. The 21st century leader is being called upon to lead in an unfamiliar world in which the once familiar maps from the Industrial Age no longer work.

We began this book with the Prologue, in which we referred to the last upgrade in the human brain which happened approximately 70,000 years ago. Will this brain serve us well as we head into a 21st century reality far more complex than anything we have known until now? Will we be relevant? What new worlds await discovery? What new maps and new abilities do we need for the 21st century? Neuroscience is demonstrating how we are born with an innate sense of compassion and care for the other. But we also carry circuits of aggression, selfishness and hate. While we are choosing to write about the former, we must acknowledge that the latter exists in equal measure.

Our hope is that this book has inspired you in some way to join a community of practitioners committed to the task of rehumanizing their leadership and their organizations. In many ways, this task is a shared journey of remembering who we are as humans. It is an invitation for all leaders to consider how they might help shape better businesses, better institutions and, ultimately, a better world.

Sudhanshu Palsule
Michael Chavez

Endnotes

1. Rifkin, Jeremy, *The Empathic Civilization: The Race to Global Consciousness in a World in Crisis*, TarcherPerigee, 2009.

2. Huffington, Arianna, *The Fourth Instinct: The Call of the Soul*, Simon & Schuster, 2003.

3. Mackey, John and Sisodia, Rajendra, *Conscious Capitalism: Liberating the Heroic Spirit of Business*, Harvard Business Review Press, 2014.

4. Veissière, Samuel, "Caring for Others is What Made Our Species Unique." *Psychology Today*, 28 October 2015.

5. Laszlo, Ervin, *Evolution: The Grand Synthesis*, Shambhala, 1987.

6. Mihalcik, Carrie, "Facebook Stock's $120 billion Loss is Biggest Single-day Drop Ever," *CNET*, 26 July 2018, https://www.cnet.com.

7. "Edelman Trust Barometer Special Report," Edelman Trust, accessed 21 October 2019, https://edelman.com.

8. "The Sustainability Imperative: New Insights on Consumer Expectations," *2015 Nielsen Global Sustainability Report*.

9. The name 'Kopernik' refers to how Nicolaus Copernicus, through his theories of a heliocentric solar system, changed the way people perceive everything.

10. Duke Corporate Education, "Leading in Context," *2013 CEO Study*.

11. Guglielmo, Frank and Palsule, Sudhanshu, *The Social Leader: Redefining Leadership for the Complex Social Age*, Routledge, 2014.

12. "Workforce of the future: The Yellow World in 2030," *PwC*, 2017.

13. Gadhia, Jayne-Anne, *The Virgin Banker*, Virgin Books, 2018.

14. Hickman, Gill Robinson and Sorensen, Georgia, *The Power of Invisible Leadership: How a Compelling Common Purpose Inspires Exceptional Leadership*, Sage Publications, 2013.

15. Jones, Bruce, "The Difference Between Purpose and Mission." *Harvard Business Review*, 2 February 2016.

16. See: Salmon, Felix, "Recipe for Disaster: The Formula that Killed Wall Street," *Wired*, 23 February 2009.

17. Frankl, Viktor, *Man's Search for Meaning*, Beacon Press, 1946.

18. Rifkin, op. cit.

19. Guglielmo and Palsule, op. cit.

20. Guglielmo and Palsule, op. cit. p. 8.

21. Seligman, Martin E.P., *Authentic Happiness: Using the New Positive Psychology to Realize Your Potential for Lasting Fulfillment*, Simon & Schuster, 2002.

22. Randall, William, *The Stories We Are: An Essay on Self-Creation*, University of Toronto Press, 1995.

23. Rukeyser, Muriel, *The Speed of Darkness* from *The Collected Poems of Muriel Rukeyser*, Random House, 1968.

24. Hardy G.H., *A Mathematician's Apology*, Cambridge University Press, 1940.

25. Denning, Steve, "The Internet Is Finally Forcing Management to Care About People." *Harvard Business Review*, 5 May 2015.

26. Denning, Stephen, *The Age of Agile: How Smart Companies are Transforming the Way Work Gets Done*, Amacom, 2018.

27. Sinek, Simon, (May 2010). "How Great Leaders Inspire Action," [Video file]. https://www.ted.com/talks/simon_sinek_how_great_leaders_inspire_action.

28. Darwin, Charles, *The Descent of Man, and Selection in Relation to Sex*, John Murray, 1871.

29. Morgan, Gareth, *Images of Organization*, Sage Publications, 1986.

30. Ibid.

31. Jensen, Michael C., and Meckling, William H., "Theory of the Firm." *Journal of Financial Economics*, 1976.

32. Bower, Joseph L., and Paine, Lynn S., "The Error at the Heart of Corporate Leadership," *Harvard Business Review*, 95, No. 3, May–June 2017.

33. "North Star: Purpose-driven Leadership for the 21st Century." *Global CEO Study, Leaders on Purpose*, Horváth & Partners, 2018.

34. Gadhia, op. cit.

35. Wilson III, Earnest J., "Empathy is Still Lacking in the Leaders Who Need It Most." *Harvard Business Review*, 21 September 2015.

36. Heimans, Jeremy and Timms, Henry, *New Power: How Power Works in Our Hyperconnected World – and How to Make it Work for You*, Pan Macmillan, 2018.

37. Heimans, Jeremy and Timms, Henry, "Understanding 'New Power',"
    Harvard Business Review, December 2014.

38. Carson, Rachel, *Silent Spring*, Houghton Mifflin, 1962.

39. Capra, Fritjof and Luisi, Pier Luigi Luisi, *The Systems View of Life: A Unifying Vision*, Cambridge University Press, 2014.

40. Guglielmo and Palsule, op. cit.

41. See: Heifetz, Ronald and Linsky, Marty, "A Survival Guide for Leaders."
    Harvard Business Review, June 2002.

42. See: Senge, Peter, *The Fifth Discipline: The Art and Practice of the Learning Organization*, Doubleday, 1990.

43. Popova, Maria, *Figuring*, Pantheon, 2019.

44. Pink, Daniel, *Drive: The Surprising Truth About What Motivates Us*,
    Riverhead Books, 2009.

45. Watts, Alan, *The Wisdom of Insecurity*, Pantheon Books, 1951.

46. Flitter, Emily and Thrush, Glenn, "Wells Fargo Said to Be Target
    of $1 Billion US Fine." *New York Times*, 19 April 2018.

47. Keltner, Dacher, *The Power Paradox: How We Gain and Lose Influence*,
    Penguin Books, 2017.

48. Hogeveen Wilfrid, Jeremy, Inzlicht, Michael and Obhi, Sukhvinder
    S., "Power Changes How the Brain Responds to Others." *Journal of Experimental Psychology*, 143, No. 2, 2014.

49. Kraus, M. W., Côté, S., & Keltner, D. "Social Class, Contextualism,
    and Empathic Accuracy," *Psychological Science*, 21, 2010.

50. Fiske, S. T., "Controlling Other People: The Impact of Power on
    Stereotyping," *American Psychologist*, 48 (6), 1993.

51. Kolind, Lars and Bøtter, Jacob, *Unboss*, Jyllands-Postens Forlag, 2012.

52. Pétrement, Simone, *Simone Weil: A Life*, (1976) trans. Raymond Rosenthal,
    Letter to Joë Bousquet, 13 April 1942.

53. Kahneman, Daniel, *Thinking, Fast and Slow*, Farrar, Straus and Giroux, 2011.

54. Kanter, Rosabeth Moss, "How Great Companies Think Differently,"
    Harvard Business Review, November 2011.

55. Tansley, Arthur J., "The Use and Abuse of Vegetational Concepts and
    Terms," *Ecology*, 16, No. 3, July 1935, pp. 284–307.

56. Carson, Rachel, op. cit. p. 51.

57. Bateson, Gregory, *Steps to an Ecology of Mind: Collected Essays in Anthropology, Psychiatry, Evolution, and Epistemology*, University
    of Chicago Press, 1972.

58. Capra, Fritjof and Luisi, Pier Luigi Luisi, op. cit.

59. "Our history," Unilever, accessed October 21, 2019,
    https://www.unilever.com/about/who-we-are/our-history/.

60. Daneshkhu, Scheherazade and Barber, Lionel, "Paul Polman: How I Fended
    Off a Hostile Takeover Bid," *Financial Times*, 3 December 2017.

61. Kanter, op. cit.

62. Edmans, Alex, "Why Purpose is Key to Corporate Success," *Forbes*, 16 May 2016.

63. Weed, Keith, "Brands Must Become Sustainable or Risk Irrelevance,"
    The Guardian, 21 March 2016.

64. Buckley, Thomas and Campbell, Matthew, "If Unilever Can't Make Feel-
    Good Capitalism Work, Who Can?" *Bloomberg Businessweek*, 31 August 2017.

65. Edelman, Richard, "Paul Polman – The CEO Who Changed Capitalism."
    www.edelman.com, 7 December 2018.

66. Shrikhande, V.N., *Reflections of a Surgeon*, Popular Prakashan, India, 2015.

67. Iacoboni, Marco, *Mirroring People: The Science of Empathy and How We
    Connect with Others*, Picador, 2009.

68. Lehrer, Jonah, "The Mirror Neuron Revolution: Explaining What Makes
    Humans Social," *Scientific American: Mind Matters*, July 2008.

69. Rifkin, op. cit.

70. Armstrong, Kim, "I Feel Your Pain: the Neuroscience of Empathy,"
    Observer (Association for Psychological Science), January 2018.

71. Colvin, Geoff, *Humans Are Underrated: What High Achievers Know That
    Brilliant Machines Never Will*, Portfolio/Penguin, 2015.

72. Ainge Roy, Eleanor, "Real Leaders Do Exist: Jacinda Ardern Uses Solace
    and Steel to Guide a Broken Nation," *The Guardian*, 19 March 2019.

73. Nussbaum, Martha, *The Monarchy of Fear: A Philosopher Looks at Our
    Political Crisis*, Simon & Schuster, 2018.

74. Li, Danny, "Governing Beyond Fear and Anger," *Slate*, 22 March 2019.

75. Ibid.

76. Bloom, Paul, *Against Empathy: The Case for Rational Compassion*, Random
    House, 2016.

77. Hougaard, Rasmus and Carter, Jacqueline, *The Mind of the Leader: How to
    Lead Yourself, Your People, and Your Organization for Extraordinary Results*,
    Harvard Business Review Press, 2018.

78. Harari, Yuval Noah, *21 Lessons for the 21st Century*, Spiegel & Grau, 2018.

79. Ikigai translates roughly as 'life that is worthwhile'. In Okinawan
    culture it is often thought of as 'a reason to get up in the morning'.
    García, Héctor and Miralles, Francesc, trans. Cleary, Heather, *Ikigai:
    The Japanese Secret to a Long and Happy Life*, Penguin Books, 2016. pp. 9-12.

80. Graham, Paul, 'How to Do What You Love', *paulgraham.com*, January 2006.

81. Dennett, Dan. (February 2002) "Dangerous Memes," [Video file]. https://www.ted.com/talks/dan_dennett_on_dangerous_memes.

82. Hawking, Stephen, *A Brief History of Time*, Bantam Books, 1998.

83. Nieto-Rodriguez, Antonio, *The Project Revolution: How to Succeed in a Project-Driven World*, LID Publishing, 2019.

84. *Project Management Job Growth and Talent Gap 2017–2027*, Project Management Institute, 2017, www.pmi.org/-/media/pmi/documents/public/pdf/learnign/job-growth-report.pdf?sc_lang_temp=eng.

85. *Pulse of the Profession 9th Global Project Management Survey: Success Rates Rise – Transforming the High Cost of Low Performance*, Project Management Institute, 2017, https://www.pmi.org/-/media/pmi/documents/public/pdf/learning/thought-leadership/pulse/pulse-of-the-profession-2017.pdf.

86. Jargon, Julie, "Chipotle Picks Taco Bell CEO Brian Niccol to Be Its New Chief," *The Wall Street Journal*, February 13, 2018.

87. Ibarra, Herminia, "The Authenticity Paradox," *Harvard Business Review*, January-February, 2015.

88. Kanter, op. cit.

89. Dietz, Doug. (May 2012). "Transforming healthcare for children and their families," [Video file]. https://www.youtube.com/watch?v=jajduxPD6H4.

90. Attributed to the late Paula Underwood, an Iroquois-American author and oral historian, who in turn attributed this quote to her father, Sharp Eyed Hawk.

91. Shaw, George Bernard, *Back to Methuselah, act I, Selected Plays with Prefaces*, vol. 2, p. 7, 1949.

92. Campbell, Joseph, edited by Osbon, Diane, *A Joseph Campbell Companion: Reflections on the Art of Living*, Harper Perennial, 1991.

About the Authors

Sudhanshu Palsule is an award-winning educator, CEO advisor and speaker and is regarded as one of the leading thinkers in the fields of Complexity and 21st Century Leadership. He teaches at Duke Corporate Education in the areas of Navigating Complexity, Leading Change and 21st Century Leadership. His current research focuses on building effective 21st century organizations that can thrive in increasingly complex global ecosystems. He is deeply passionate about rehumanizing leadership in a 21st century context of accelerating change and complex global problems in a deeply divisive world.

Professor Palsule is also a Senior Associate at The Møller Institute, University of Cambridge. He has been teaching for more than three decades at several leading universities and business schools including INSEAD. Author of several books, his most recent one was *The Social Leader: Redefining Leadership for the Complex Social Age.*

He has lived and taught in four continents and has worked in the private sector and at the United Nations. Originally trained as a quantum physicist, his work on leadership draws upon new research from neurology and psychology and his own exploration of human behaviour and the workings of the mind.

Michael Chavez is the CEO for Duke Corporate Education, part of Duke University and the premier global provider of leadership development solutions.

He teaches, facilitates and advises in the areas of Leadership and Culture, Organizational Networks, Team Collaboration, Strategy and Execution. His research focuses on how leaders can most effectively shape, institutionalize and lead from a shared organizational purpose. Based on his work, Michael believes that by engaging people around a purpose, shared meaning and empathy, leaders can create the foundation for better business, and greater sustainability, in a complex world.

Michael has more than 25 years of experience in the fields of executive management, strategy, marketing, customer analytics, and organizational learning and development. His corporate experience at The Coca-Cola Company and the *Los Angeles Times*, coupled with his background in strategy consulting and technology, inspired him to pursue a career in leadership and organizational development. He has led projects all over the world and in a variety of industries, including technology, pharmaceuticals, consumer products, retail, financial services and media.